women behind BARS

CHILE'S ABORTION LAWS

A HUMAN RIGHTS ANALYSIS

women behind BARS

Published by:
The Center for Reproductive Law & Policy
120 Wall Street
New York, NY 10005
USA
http://www.crlp.org

The Open Forum on Reproductive Health and Rights
(*Foro Abierto de Salud y Derechos Reproductivos*)
Purisma 160-E., Recoleta
Santiago, Chile
forosalu@entelchile.net

Design and production by Deborah Dudley

ISBN 1-890671-15-0

ACKNOWLEDGMENTS

This report was coproduced by the Open Forum on Reproductive Health and Rights in Chile (Open Forum) and the Center for Reproductive Law and Policy (CRLP) in New York. Lidia Casas Becerra conducted the research for and wrote the first draft of this report. Verónica Matus and Lorena Fríes, consulting attorneys to the Open Forum, edited it. Viviana Waisman, consulting attorney to the CRLP, wrote the chapter on human rights. Viviana Waisman, consulting attorney, Gaby Oré Aguilar and Katherine Hall Martinez, staff attorneys with CRLP's International Program, edited the final version. Dr. María Isabel Matamala Vivaldi, deputy coordinator of the Latin American and Caribbean Women's Health Network, wrote the preface and acted as peer reviewer.

The following individuals affiliated with the Open Forum collaborated in the coordination and production of this report: Josefina Hurtado, Rosa Ferrada, and Mireya Zuleta, coordinators of the Open Forum; Francisca Perez, former coordinator of the Open Forum; and Verónica Vergara, secretary to the Open Forum. Marisol Matus, Camila Maturana, Mónica Cheuquian, and Marcela Olea assisted with research in several cities. Gloria Salazar did the 1996 interview featured in this report. Angélica Vergara collaborated in the drafting of the chapter on public health.

The following people affiliated with CRLP collaborated in the coordination and production of the report: Catherine Albisa, former CRLP staff attorney and consulting attorney to CRLP; Alison-Maria Bartolone and Lisa Hibler, International Program assistants; and Cynthia Eyakuze, International Program associate. Julieta Lemaitre, consultant, translated the report to English, and Katherine Hall Martinez edited the translated version. Deborah Dudley of CRLP designed and produced the report.

PREFACE

This publication examines Chilean society, raising doubts about the humanity of its development, and challenges Chile's public policies. It is a book that lays bare incontrovertible facts, facts that have remained hidden under the dust of court records and the blanket of prevailing hypocrisy. National and international discourses on equality, gender, and poverty are confronted by these facts, which reveal the dramatic gender and class inequality in our country. But in the void left by need, rights and their protection are nothing but a mere abstraction.

The investigators place us face to face with 159 low-income women, with little formal education and in low-paying jobs, who were punished for making the same choice that 150,000 Chilean women make every year: the decision to terminate their pregnancy. By penalizing abortion, the Chilean legal system fails 400 women each day. They are punished because as poor women, neither their formal education, their work environment, their personal relationships nor the power structure allow them access to preventive measures or other health services.

This punishment is superimposed over the daily deprivation that society has given them as their due for as long as they can remember. They most likely regard such inequality of opportunity as "natural." They—especially those who are not part of the world of paid labor—are on the other side of a window that is less and less transparent, rendering them invisible, erasing them, casting them aside and leaving them excluded from the other world, an injustice more closely tied to the institutionalized systems of control and punishment day by day. When one is condemned to contribute little or nothing to society, the effort to exercise one's rights becomes endless and futile.

This report is also a testimony to solidarity among women, to those who seek to understand and give shelter to other women, giving them the chance to be visible, to be seen as human beings. Exposed in this report are the paradoxes that Chilean society at the end of the century needs to resolve.

It is possible to be responsible in regard to both population dynamics and the possibility of offering a dignified life and rights to those who are born. Without question, the women featured in this report knew nothing of population dynamics; but surely they did know of affection and disaffection, of the immediate risks of their decision to have an abortion and the future risks for those who are born into the lack of opportunities, lack of rights, lack of love, and lack of hope that characterizes their lives.

Is it responsible and fair to expect a woman to give birth on command, when she is unable to offer the prospect of a future to the newly born, because the necessary social conditions are lacking? The answer is evident in a country where only 44% of births are planned, and which has the highest abortion rate in Latin America. The answer is all the more evident when we see that during every year covered in this research, anonymous and powerless women have been sacrificial lambs to the inner contradictions of one of the more regressive and useless pieces of legislation in the world today.

When public health services include as a primary objective the improvement of the quality of health services, does it make sense that it is their employees who present almost all of the reports to the police for abortion complications? The figures are irrefutable, as is the gender and class inequality that they reveal.

It would be necessary to investigate further what it is that institutions whose objective is to promote and ensure everyone's well-being are seeking to punish, to discern what can invert the role of health services to the point where they judge and condemn the suffering women who went to them to save their own lives. Maybe in the metaphorical world of those who report them to the police, women's sexuality is linked to filth and abomination. Perhaps in their cultural codes the divorce between sexuality and parenthood is impermissible only where women are concerned. In all likelihood, they have learned to accept gender inequalities as normal.

In spite of the fact that almost two-thirds of the women prosecuted in the four cities studied did not have access to defense counsel, and in spite of the scandalous violation of rights that this implies, there is no institutional shame. No one in society or in the judicial system has apologized to these women. These incidents are of no interest to the mass media. These women were left defenseless, forgotten, submerged in their class and gender imprisonment. In spite of the rhetoric of equality, their rights as citizens were not valued.

The Open Forum on Reproductive Health and Rights and the Center for

Reproductive Law and Policy have together succeeded in bringing women prosecuted for abortion to this side of the window, revealing the injustices to which they have been subjected and opening the debate from another angle. In this way, the investigators, with their conscientious construction of facts, are making a decisive contribution to the argument.

Will the social, political, and cultural conditions that impede or limit women's exercise of their sexual and reproductive rights ever be modified? Will ideological guardianship ever cease, and will the diversity that exists in our country be accepted? Will women continue to be criminalized in spite of international consensus? Will the country continue to turn away, trying to excuse silences and omissions under the pretext that legislating on abortion carries too high a political cost? Will poor women continue to be taken to prison when they seek medical attention in public health establishments after risking their lives to obtain an abortion?

We hope that this book's invitation to an inclusive and open debate contributes to cultural and political changes that will humanize our country and make it a truly modern one.

Dr. María Isabel Matamala Vivaldi, Deputy Coordinator, Latin American and Caribbean Women's Health Network

CONTENTS

EXECUTIVE SUMMARY

Court records of women prosecuted for obtaining or inducing their own abortion and of women and men arrested for abortion-related offenses reveal that Chilean law violates the human rights of these individuals. Moreover, the actions of Chile's public employees in implementing these laws constitute a violation of the human rights of women who terminate their pregnancies and those who assist them to do so. In Chile, abortion is not permissible in any circumstance, not even to save the life of the pregnant woman. This restrictive law violates women's reproductive rights, including their right to health, their right to liberty and security, as well as potentially their right to life. In addition to the rights violated by the prohibition itself, the methods by which women are reported to the police, and the criminal process they, abortion providers, and "accomplices" undergo violate numerous other human rights, such as the right to due process, the right to privacy, and the right of a criminal defendant to be afforded an attorney. This study sheds light on these numerous violations and makes recommendations to Chile as well as to the international community to take action to end these grave violations of human rights.

Using information contained in court records, this study documents and profiles women, abortion providers, and other "accomplices" who were prosecuted for abortion in four cities in Chile during two periods, 1983-84 and 1990–91. The former period was during the military dictatorship; the latter took place during the period of Chile's transition to a democratically elected government. In addition to examining the criminal laws employed to prosecute these individuals, the investigation includes a breakdown by city and gender of those prosecuted under the abortion laws. Furthermore, this study examines the legal framework of Chile's abortion laws, as well as the criminal procedure that is involved in these prosecutions. Also included is a socioeconomic profile of the women and the providers included in the study.

HUMAN RIGHTS IMPLICATIONS OF THE STUDY

The Instigation of Prosecutions

Most of the criminal prosecutions of women who had obtained abortions were commenced following reports to the police by the public hospitals where they sought treatment for abortion-related complications. In this study, public hospitals accounted for 92% of the institutions that reported women to the police for abortions and 80% of the total number of reports to the police. Notably, none of the prosecutions was instigated by private hospitals or clinics. As a result of the denunciations of women by public health facilities, a disproportionate number of low-income women are prosecuted for obtaining abortions. This violates the right to nondiscrimination based on a person's economic status provided for in the Covenant on Civil and Political Rights and the International Covenant on Economic, Social, and Cultural Rights.

Much of the information provided by the women to the hospital staff was recorded in their medical records. Medical personnel who suspected that a woman had undergone an abortion often informed the police. The criteria used to determine whether to report these women was unclear and seemingly arbitrary. In all cases, the women who were reported had low incomes. Some women were placed under arrest when they were at the hospital, while others were interrogated there. In the cases where women were transferred directly from the hospital to the courts, their poor health condition was often recorded in the judicial records examined in this study. Other women were reported through "hospital procedures." The procedures used by the doctors, nurses, and midwives who reported women who had obtained abortions to the police are more reminiscent of police interrogation methods than of the professionalism of health care workers who should have been focused on the care of injured women. These health care providers forced many women to "confess" that they had obtained abortions by threatening to withhold medical care if they did not. Sometimes an oral confession was obtained. But, prior to receiving medical attention, at least one female patient was made to sign a written "confession" dictated by the doctor to the midwife or nurse assisting him.

Several women in this study reported that they had been abused by health providers in the hospitals. One woman explained that she "confessed" to having obtained an abortion after being badly treated by the attending physician. Another woman had been admitted to the hospital because she was experiencing symptoms that signaled a possible miscarriage. After the symptoms subsided, she requested an immediate release from the hospital because she had three small children at home who required her care. The doctor released her but warned her not to return. Later at home, the woman suffered a miscarriage and had to return to the hospital. The doctor subsequently reported her to the police. The treatment of these women by the health providers at these public hospitals not only violates these women's right to health and their reproductive rights, but it also violates their right to doctor-patient confidentiality.

Approximately 13% of the reports to the police were filed by individuals that were neither hospital nor police employees. These individuals were most likely to be family members (45%) or the women's partners (35%). The men who reported their partners to the police were often motivated by revenge, usually because the woman had separated from the man and the relationship had not ended on good terms. Often, these men turned to the police without any regard for the consequences of their actions; frequently, they had participated in either the decision to obtain an abortion or in the abortion procedure itself.

Women's Access to Legal Representation

This study reveals that a significant number of the women prosecuted for undergoing abortions were not afforded legal representation. On average, only 38% of the women were represented by an attorney, while 60% of the women were not represented by an attorney at any stage of the prosecution. This lack of representation violates the right of a criminal defendant to legal counsel under both national and international laws.

Some women experienced other human rights violations once in custody. Two women in this study testified in court that they were mistreated by the police. One woman testified that she was made to undress and then a woman, presumably a police officer, examined her and told her that it would be best if she told the truth because in any case, she was still pregnant, and that if she did not talk, her parents would go to jail. The other woman who was mistreated by the police had been admitted to the maternity ward of the hospital with symptoms of a miscarriage. She told her attorney that in the Division of Sexual Crimes she was badly treated and was pressured to testify as to "what she had done to herself." It turned out that she had suffered a prolapsed uterus that might have caused her miscarriage.

Punishment and Pretrial Custody

It is relatively common in Chile that a person suspected of a crime remains in custody for a period of time before trial. The results of this study seem to indicate that pretrial custody is used to "punish" the accused even though she or he has not yet been convicted. Fifty-seven percent of the women who underwent abortions, 87% of providers and "principal-participants," and 87% of accomplices spent time in prison. It is particularly problematic for a judge to order a woman who obtained an abortion or an "accomplice" to be held in prison prior to trial on the basis that he or she is a flight risk or could be "dangerous" to others. Those accused of being "accomplices" to an abortion spent an average of 20.5 days in pretrial custody, the women who obtained abortions spent an average of 31.3 days in pretrial custody, those accused of being "principals" in the crime (the person who induced the woman to obtain an abortion) spent an average of 68.5 days in pretrial custody, and the providers spent an average of 84.1 days in pretrial custody. The procedure followed in the prosecution of these individuals violates both their right to due process as well as their right to be presumed innocent.

Judges may sometimes view the situation of the women who obtain abortions with more compassion due to the often dire situations that led these women to seek an abortion. However, the actions of the providers are viewed differently. Providers are generally perceived as performing abortions for profit, when, in actuality, many of the providers in this study were often women who performed the abortions free of charge as a service to low-income women without resources to obtain a safer abortion but who were desperate to end an unwanted pregnancy.

PROFILE OF THE WOMEN WHO HAD ABORTIONS

Of the women included in this study who were prosecuted for having an abortion, 61% were between the ages of 18 and 29. Women between the ages of 30 and 41 represented 26% of those profiled; five of the women (8%) were under 18-years-old. Not all of the women included in this study were prosecuted. Five women under the age of 18 were not prosecuted, and four other women testified that they underwent abortions without giving their consent.

Approximately 49% of the women who obtained abortions did not have a partner. This figure includes women who were separated from their spouses (4%), widows (1%), and single women (44%). However, 43% of the women did have a partner. The educational level of the women in this study was harder to document given the fact that most court records simply noted whether the woman prosecuted was literate. In general, the conclusion can be drawn that the majority of the women prosecuted for abortion tended not to have a high level of education. Approximately 7% of the women were illiterate, and 21% of the women had not completed primary school. An additional 21% could "read and write." About 19% had attended some years of high school, but did not graduate. The study was only able to confirm that 9% of the women had finished high school.

Most of the women profiled in this study, approximately 60%, had either one or two children at the time of their abortion. Women with three children represented about 16% of those prosecuted. About 47% of the women who had abortions worked, while 41% were not wage earners (mostly housewives [29%] and students [12%]). Of the women who worked, 22% were domestic workers.

PROFILE OF ABORTION PROVIDERS

Overall, this study reveals that the abortion providers who were prosecuted tended to be other women (79%), who were often as low-income as the women seeking abortions. When the providers were men, they tended to use bolder methods, involving medical instruments, for example, and they usually had some training in the health field.

CONCLUSION

The findings of this investigation demonstrate that the restrictive abortion laws in Chile violate numerous human rights protected by national laws as well as by regional and international human rights instruments. Among those rights violated are the right to health; the right to life, liberty, and security; the right to be free of discrimination based on gender and socioeconomic status; the right to reproductive health and family planning; the right to privacy; the right to legal representation; the right to due process; and the right to be presumed innocent. Women with few economic resources and little education are typically the victims of unsafe procedures. Whatever their reasons for making the difficult decision not to bear a child, it is these women who are typically subjected to criminal prosecution and, often, imprisonment.

FOREWORD

Interview with Carmen
June 5, 1996

Carmen was born in a small town in the southern region of the country, the fifth of six children in a peasant family. At 12 she began to work as a maid in a private home. Carmen worked in various homes in Santiago and in other cities as well.

> I stayed four to six months in each house. I didn't last too long even when I had good bosses, and if they were bad, I didn't last longer than two weeks.

At 16 she had a boyfriend, the neighbor of her older sister.

> We didn't see each other much, because I was always going from one place to the next ... and then ... I got pregnant ... by accident. I was 17, going on 18. It was a good relationship. When I knew I was pregnant, we had broken up already, but he came back when he found out I was pregnant. But after five months of pregnancy we broke up for good. He was just a kid....

At first, Carmen's boyfriend denied he was the baby's father. Later on he accepted it, although he never legally recognized the child as his. After the child's birth, Carmen went back to Santiago, where she worked shifts in a factory.

After that, Carmen had two other boyfriends. She got pregnant again.

> I don't even know how it happened. We had been going out for a year. But we went out just for fun, not for the future, just for fun.... We liked each other.

Although at various times she had used contraceptives, such as oral contraceptives and injections she got in the pharmacy without any orientation or information, this time she didn't apply what she knew about contraception.

> I knew I could get pregnant but I took the risk. Sometimes you don't think of the consequences.... I didn't know what to do. I didn't want anybody to find out. I knew I was pregnant and right away I told myself I can't do this, because with the child it was already too difficult. I was helping my sister, I was helping her

> pay the rent. We lived alone, but after my first child was born we both had to worry about him, and unfortunately they told me the child was epileptic. I closed up.

Carmen thought of having an abortion.

> I went over to the woman and I told her I knew she did these things. And that I was pregnant and needed her help. And she told me everything I had to bring and where to buy it. I bought the things and took them to her: a surgeon's probe, cotton, alcohol.... When I went back to her, she put the probe in and told me to take something for the infection. But the probe came out in the afternoon....

Carmen had a difficult afternoon and night.

> In the morning when I got up I felt sick, I had a strong contraction, and I went to the bathroom, and everything came out really quickly. I had so many feelings inside, I didn't know what to do. I didn't tell anybody. The only thing I remember is I started to work and I felt well physically, I didn't have a fever or anything.

The toilet was clogged and she called the plumber, who showed up after two days.

> The plumber came, unclogged the toilet, and everything was there. He even called me and I didn't say anything and kept on as if nothing had happened. Then the boss came and I told her what the plumber had found, but I didn't say who had done it. She thought of her daughter's friends, also of a girl I had brought over, but never thought of me.

Carmen's boss immediately called the police, after interrogating all the women in the house except for Carmen: "I don't know if she had a feeling it had been me or if she trusted me." She also called her brother, who was a lawyer and a politician, and he came over quickly.

> The police came and also a very rude woman. I told the police I hadn't done anything, because I had thrown away the probe and everything. They told me to say I hadn't noticed anything. I said I had been pregnant but that I hadn't done it to myself. I denied it until ... I talked with Don Sergio.... When the boss's brother came, he told them to leave us alone, and he talked with me, and

I told him what had happened.

She was taken to the Police Station, where she told them the facts. She didn't know the exact address of the place where she had had the probe inserted, but she knew how to get there. They took her there and they told her to knock on the door with the pretext of paying what she owed for the procedure. She did so and the woman who had performed the abortion was also arrested, causing a great commotion in the neighborhood. "They came out from everywhere, insulting me and supporting her." Carmen was later taken to the Emergency Room, and from there she was sent to Salvador Hospital. She was hospitalized there and the lining of her uterus was scraped even though there were no signs of infection. She was in custody all the time. Carmen felt the auxiliary personnel at the hospital tried to extend her stay there, to keep her from having to spend too long in jail.

> The policeman was there day and night. Yes, day and night, standing there by the door all day and all night.

Carmen was in jail for three months. When she was taken to court with other prisoners, she was separated from them, because there was concern about retaliation from the woman who had performed the abortion, who was also in the same prison.

> When they called me at first, I got in the car and the other women all jumped on me so the guards took me out and put me in the back, because the other one said she knew people inside, so they took me and put me in the back.

A lawyer from the Legal Aid Corporation was in charge of her case.

> ... because in the beginning it was Don Sergio, but since he is against abortion and is a public figure, how could he defend me?... So at the end it was someone from the corporation, but I think he didn't do anything, Don Sergio did more making phone calls. The lawyer — I don't think he did anything, because he never called me to say, Hey, listen, this is going like this. Really he never said anything, because what I knew was what my boss would have someone tell me, but he never said: Your case is going this way. I knew everything through my boss.

One day she got a message from her boss, telling her she would be out of jail the next Monday. Her boss was waiting for her in court, after paying the bail.

> When I got out of there, I thought it was all a lie, like I was still locked in. For the next three days I was still feeling locked in.

She decided to travel to her mother's house.

> After I got there they didn't ask me anything. I don't know if it was for better or worse. No one said anything. Not my mother or my brother. No one ever said anything. I really don't know if I would have wanted them to ask me or not.

Carmen's experience changed her relationship with her boss.

> Suddenly she'll start in on it, she'll ask about it, then she'll do the same thing.... And when I ask permission to go out for the weekend, she gives me permission and says remember not to get pregnant or not to go to bed with somebody. So sometimes we clash and I wish I could leave.... I'm grateful, and I will always be grateful, but I'm not going to thank her every day for what she did for me. Always when people do something for you they want you to stay with them. So she wants me to stay with her forever and never to say anything that bothers her, because of what she did.

Excerpted from an interview conducted by Gloria Salazar

INTRODUCTION

The Chilean abortion law is one of the most restrictive in the world. It prohibits the procedure without exception, even in order to save the life of the pregnant woman. Among Latin American countries, Chile shares this distinction with El Salvador.

It is estimated that in the first five years of the 1990s there were approximately 44 million abortions worldwide. Close to 4 million occurred in Latin America.[1] In contrast with North America, Europe, and some Asian countries, in Latin America, because abortion is illegal, there are no reliable statistics. In 1990, there were around 160,000 abortions in Chile, while in Mexico there were 533,000 in the same year, and in Brazil in 1991 there were 1,433,000 abortions. In the beginning of the 1990s, there were 5.5 abortions for every 10 births in Chile, while in Brazil there were 4.4 for every 10 and in Mexico 2.1 abortions for every 10 births.[2] The per capita number of abortions in Chile remains one of the highest in the continent, and constitutes one of the main causes of maternal mortality in that country.[3]

In Latin America beginning in the 1970s, both public policy and couples began to agree with the goal of having smaller families than in previous decades.[4] The average size of the family in the region has decreased almost 50%, from close to six children per woman in the 1960s to a little more than three today.[5]

Directly related to this drop is the fact that contraceptive prevalence has increased considerably in most Latin American countries as a result of the implementation of family planning policies. At present in Latin America, the responsibility for family planning falls primarily on women. The most popular contraceptives are the pill, intrauterine devices, and female sterilization. Traditional contraceptive methods such as abstinence during periods of greatest fertility are also present in the region.[6] In Chile, among women of reproductive age (between 15 and 44 years of age), 56% use contraceptive methods to avoid unwanted pregnancies, while in Colombia, Peru, Mexico, and Bolivia the numbers vary between 34% and 44%.[7]

Nevertheless, a great portion of women do not have their family planning needs met. Social and cultural circumstances, such as inaccessibility and poor quality of services, lack of economic resources, fear of secondary effects, and the almost nonexistent use of condoms by men, among other reasons, hinder women's ability to access contraceptive methods. In addition, contraceptives are not 100% effective, and some women, for various reasons, do not use them correctly. Huge numbers of women cannot or do not use contraceptives, resulting in a high level of unwanted pregnancies and abortions.

From a human rights perspective, the lack of access to family planning methods, and its most obvious consequence, unwanted pregnancies terminated by abortions, shows that sexual freedom and reproductive rights are still not fully protected or guaranteed for Chilean women. Furthermore, the fact that in Chile and in various countries in the region abortion is a crime, places a large group of women at risk of resorting to dangerous abortion procedures. This violates the most fundamental of human rights, the right to life and physical and psychological integrity.

A. OBJECTIVES OF THIS REPORT

This report is the result of a collaborative effort between the Open Forum on Reproductive Health and Rights in Chile and the Center for Reproductive Law and Policy in New York. It is the second part of a research effort of which the first part, *Women Prosecuted for Abortion*,[8] was previously published in Spanish. That report dealt with the social and economic profile of women who were prosecuted and imprisoned for abortion in Santiago. In this second part, the research was decentralized to include data from cities as diverse as Arica, Valparaiso, Temuco, and Santiago. In this second phase of the research, in contrast with the first part, court records for abortion, rather than legal aid files, in the years selected for the research, were analyzed, whatever the form of defense. Moreover, the report identifies human rights violations based on Chilean laws and international treaties ratified by the Chilean government. This report also shows the socioeconomic profile of the actors involved in the termination of the pregnancy, as well as that of the women who obtained the abortions.

The first chapter of this report analyzes the way in which various restrictive abortion laws and the judicial process itself violate various human rights. The second chapter focuses on abortion as a public health problem, establishing the relationship between population policies and health programs and their impact on women's mortality rates and on the frequency of abortion in Chile. The third and fourth chapters present the status of abortion in Chile, starting with an analysis of the current legal framework and reviewing each step in the criminal process and the socioeconomic variables that the cases demonstrate. The last chapter contains recommendations.

B. METHODOLOGY

This report is limited by the restrictions inherent in researching a hidden and criminalized reality. Both quantitative and qualitative forms of research were used. The quantitative aspect was of particular importance, since it was the basis for examining those included in the study and the construction of the profile of them. Qualitative techniques were used to delve more deeply into the stories of these women, into their choices, the circumstances that surrounded the termination of their pregnancy, the way in which it was done, the experience of the criminal process and jail, and in general, the consequences of having been subjected to a criminal process.

The research consisted of two stages: the first considered 132 court cases between 1977 and 1995 in the Metropolitan Region of Santiago, the results of which, as previously stated, were published in 1996. The second stage consisted of the analysis of a discontinuous period of four years: two in the 1980s and two at the beginning of the 1990s: that is, the years, 1983, 1984, 1990, and 1991. The reason for selecting the first two years was the high rates of penalization of abortion observed in that period, when Chilean society was characterized by strong political repression accompanied by economic crisis, high unemployment, and social instability. The latter two years — the first two years of the democratic government — were chosen as control years for comparative purposes. The 1990s have seen important political changes in Chilean society. In the context of the transition to democracy, police repression has declined and both political stability and stable economic growth has increased.

Three of the most important cities in Chile apart from the metropolitan region of Santiago (which was considered in the previous study) were chosen for this study: the cities of Arica, Valparaiso, and Temuco. This research included all the cases tried before courts in these three cities during the designated years. For Santiago, however, different parameters were established. The Metropolitan Region has two courts of appeals: Santiago and Pedro Aguirre Cerda, together including a total of 41 courts with criminal jurisdiction. In recent years, four new criminal courts were created in the jurisdictional territory of the Santiago Court of Appeals. The criminal courts that correspond to the Santiago Court of Appeals were chosen because they have a judicial archive of court records that is better organized and more functional for this kind of research than that of the Pedro Aguirre Cerda Court of Appeals, and because the Santiago Court of Appeals covers a much larger territory. In 1991, this court had 26 criminal courts under its jurisdiction, while the Pedro Aguirre Cerda Court of Appeals covered a smaller territory and had only 11 criminal courts under its jurisdiction. Within the 26 courts under the jurisdiction of the Santiago Court of Appeals, those courts were chosen that, according to the National Institute of Statistics, had had the highest quantity of abortion cases: the Fourth, Ninth, Tenth, Eighth, Nineteenth, Twenty-fourth, Twenty-fifth, and Twenty-sixth Criminal Courts. The territory covered by these courts includes the following regional areas of the city: Santiago, Central Station, Navia Hill, Pudahuel, Lo Prado, Quinta Normal, Renca, Quilicura, Lampa Colina, and La Florida.

Regarding the organization of the judicial system in the other cities, in 1991, Arica had four criminal courts that had jurisdiction in Arica, the adjacent territories, towns, and the eastern highland valleys. In Valparaiso, there were seven criminal courts, whose jurisdiction included the city of Viña del Mar. Temuco had four courts for the city and nearby rural localities.

The sample reflected in this study comprises 159 cases of women who had abortions in Santiago, Valpariaso, Arica, and Temuco, corresponding to the cases registered in the years 1983, 1984, 1990, and 1991, as set out in Table 1. Another 39 people included in the study were tried as coprincipals or providers, 8 as participants, and 15 as accomplices (Table 5). For a detailed explanation of the collection and recording of data, as well as of the difficulties encountered in this research, see Annex I.

Table 1: Sample of Cases by Year and City

	Santiago	Valparaíso	Arica	Temuco	Total
1983	15	5	4	6	30
1984	64	9	10	2	85
1990	9	8	3	7	27
1991	5	9	1	2	17
Total	93	31	18	17	159

From an interview by the Open Forum on September 25, 1997, in the "Chin Chin" prison facility in Puerto Montt, Chile. On that date, there were 22 women imprisoned there for abortion-related offenses, who were accused of having abortions or providing abortions to other women.

Adelina, 38-years-old, is head of her household and works on a fish farm, where her job is to feed salmon from a raft in the ocean near Puerto Montt, a rural sector of the coast. She has three children whom she supports, and she got pregnant without planning to. Since her life was already extremely hard without adding other expenses, she made the difficult decision to induce her own abortion by drinking a potion of herbs that some friends had recommended. But to make sure it worked, she doubled the dosage, which resulted in an intense hemorrhage and other complications, almost killing her .

CHAPTER I:
ABORTION AND HUMAN RIGHTS

The punitive and restrictive abortion laws and policies in Chile are a violation of women's human rights when examined in light of the norms contained in numerous international human rights treaties. Moreover, they are not a solution to the public health problem of abortion, which principally affects the poorest and most vulnerable women of the population.

Abortion in Chile is absolutely illegal. There are no legal exceptions to this rule, not even when abortion is the only way to save the woman's life. Some legal systems where abortion is illegal in all other circumstances recognize the defense of "necessity," an exception that patients and medical personnel can interpose when at trial. In order to interpose this defense, the accused must prove that continuing with the pregnancy presented an imminent risk to the patient's life, and that an abortion was the only way to save it. It is highly improbable that this defense would be successful in a Chilean court, since the law expressly prohibits abortion in all circumstances, and, as will be explained in Chapter III, the intention of the legislature was to eliminate all defenses that could be invoked to undercut this prohibition.

Because of this absolute prohibition on abortion, women whose lives are endangered by their pregnancy or by carrying the pregnancy to term cannot have a legal therapeutic abortion. Furthermore, many women who have suffered sexual violence or who are forced by their circumstances to terminate an unwanted pregnancy have to turn to clandestine abortions, with great risk to their health and sometimes to their life.

In this chapter the evolution of the protection of reproductive rights is briefly explained. In addition, the chapter describes the reasons that the absolute prohibition on abortion in Chile, as well as the criminal cases that result from this prohibition, constitutes a violation not only of health-related human rights, but also of other human rights, such as the right to be free from discrimination based on socioeconomic status, the right to life, liberty, and security, the right to be free from discrimination based on sex, the right to reproductive health and family planning, the right to privacy, the right to legal representation, the right to due process, and the right to be presumed innocent.

A. THE EVOLUTION OF REPRODUCTIVE RIGHTS AS HUMAN RIGHTS

The dynamic nature of human rights has allowed different sectors of society to work toward ensuring that their needs are incorporated within the international system for the protection of human rights. This dynamism has also allowed for the enrichment of the definition of human rights, allowing for an expansion of the framework of human rights protection to cover situations that particularly affect women, or that affect women differently. In this way, reproductive rights have been incorporated into the definition of human rights.

The elimination of all forms of discrimination against women has been an important basis for the expansion of international human rights to encompass the protection of reproductive rights. Discrimination on the basis of gender is prohibited by the Universal Declaration of Human Rights,[9] the International Covenant on Civil and Political Rights ("Covenant on Civil and Political Rights"),[10] the International Covenant of Economic, Social, and Cultural Rights ("Covenant on Economic and Social Rights")[11] and the American Convention on Human Rights. In 1979 the Convention on the Elimination of All Forms of Discrimination Against Women ("Women's Convention") set out a specific legal framework to protect women from discrimination. To date, this instrument has been ratified by more than 160 countries.[12]

These treaties contain the basis for the development of women's reproductive rights. The rights set forth in these treaties, such as the right to life, liberty, and security, the right to privacy, to marry and to found a family, as well as the right to be free from torture or other cruel, inhuman, or degrading treatment, are basic to the analysis of the rights of Chilean women who decide to have an abortion.

On a regional level, the Interamerican Convention on the Prevention, Punishment, and Elimination of Violence Against Women ("Convention of Belém do Pará") protects a fundamental reproductive right: freedom from sexual violence.

In addition to the international treaties intended to eliminate discrimination against women, the promotion of women's human rights occupies an important place in the history of the world conferences convoked by the United Nations. In 1968 member states recognized the importance of women's rights in the International Conference on Human Rights (the "Teheran Conference"). The final act of this conference included a section dedicated to measures to promote women's rights.[13] This conference also recognized for the first time parents' right to "determine freely and responsibly the number and spacing of their children."[14] Four years after the Teheran Conference, the General Assembly of the United Nations declared that 1975 would be the International Year for Women. The Assembly also convoked a world conference in Mexico with the goal of improving women's conditions, and declared the decade of 1976–1985 the United Nations Decade for Women. Two other world conferences were convoked during the decade for women: the World Conference of the United Nations Decade for Women: Equality, Development and Peace, held in Copenhagen in 1980, and the World Conference to Review and Appraise the Achievements of the U.N. Decade for Women: Equality, Development and Peace, which took place in Nairobi in 1985.

Among more recent conferences, the World Conference on Human Rights, held in Vienna in June, 1993, represented an important step in the way violations against women's and girls' right to equality were regarded from a human rights perspective.[15] In 1994, the World Conference on Population and Development in Cairo (the "Cairo Conference") took place. The Programme of Action of the International Conference on Population and Development (the "Cairo Programme of Action") is the conference document that, more than any other previous document related to population and development issues, emphasizes women's human rights. The international consensus expressed in this document defines reproductive health as "a state of complete physical, mental, and social well-being and not merely the absence of disease or infirmity, in all matters relating to the reproductive system and to its functions and processes."[16] It adds that "reproductive health therefore implies that people are able to have a satisfying and safe sex life and that they have the capability to reproduce and the freedom to decide if, when, and how often to do so." Men and women have the right to "obtain information" and have "access to safe, effective, affordable, and acceptable methods" of their choice for the regulation of fertility, as well as "the right of access to appropriate, adequate health care services that will enable women to go safely through pregnancy and childbirth."[17]

The Cairo Programme of Action recognizes a category of human rights known as "reproductive rights," which includes the fundamental rights of all persons to freely and responsibly choose the number and spacing of their children, and to have access to the information, education, and the means to do so. The Cairo Programme of Action repeats the same prohibition on the use of abortion as a method of family planning as the 1984 Conference on Population in Mexico had previously done. However, it also urges member nations to consider the prevention of unwanted pregnancies a priority, so that the need to resort to abortion will be reduced through the provision of more and better-quality family planning services, and that women with unwanted pregnancies have access to trustworthy information and compassionate counseling, and that in those cases where an abortion has taken place, that it be immediately followed by counseling on family planning methods.[18] The Cairo Programme of Action also provides that women must, in all cases, have access to quality health care services to treat the complications that might arise from abortion.[19]

The Fourth Conference on Women in Beijing in 1995 (the "Beijing Conference") resulted in the approval of the Beijing Declaration and the Platform for Action of the Fourth World Conference on Women (the "Beijing Platform"), which confirms the reproductive rights established in the Cairo Programme of Action. The Beijing documents also advance the discussion on sexuality that began at the Cairo Conference, introducing for the first time the concept of sexual rights. In addition, the Beijing Platform urges governments to "consider reviewing laws containing punitive measures against women who have undergone illegal abortions."[20]

This review shows that although women's health and reproductive rights have historically been a part of the concept of women's human rights, it was between 1992 and 1996 that nations participating in various international conferences made a commitment to take these rights to a new level. The documents signed by governments in these conferences do not create binding legal obligations on the part of the signatories, but they are important nonetheless because they establish key concepts and act as political action documents, setting the direction of the development of human rights.

B. INTERNATIONAL HUMAN RIGHTS VIOLATED BY CHILE'S ABORTION LAWS AND IN THE CRIMINAL PROCESS

Governments in general, and the Chilean government in particular, are obligated to respect the human rights established in international treaties that the country has ratified. Thus, people are protected not only by domestic law but also by the regional and universal human rights system. The obligations created by international law must be observed within the territory of each state as provided by that state's law. Since the 1980 constitutional reforms, article 5 of the Chilean Constitution has provided that:

> The exercise of sovereignty is limited by respect for the essential rights that emanate from human nature. It is the duty of State organs to respect and promote the rights guaranteed by the Constitution, as well as by international human rights treaties that have been ratified by Chile and have entered into force.

In Chile, in order to ratify an international treaty, both the president and Congress must agree to do so.[21] Even though the law clearly establishes the process for approving and ratifying an international treaty, there is no clear and unambiguous provision specifying the process for incorporating an international treaty into national law.[22] In spite of the absence of such a provision, the recurrent practice in Chilean courts has been to accept international treaties as domestic law as long as the following three elements are present: the treaty has been approved by Congress; it has been promulgated by presidential decree; and the Official Digest has published both the text of the treaty and that of the presidential decree that promulgates it.[23]

Although the law does not expressly provide for the legal status of a treaty, the legal status of international treaties in Chile is equivalent to that of a domestic law.[24] This can be inferred from the fact that the Constitutional Court is charged with deciding on constitutional issues that might be raised while a treaty is being considered by Congress.[25] Thus, treaties need not be submitted to an examination of their legality, since they are at least equivalent to other law.[26]

Chile has ratified all international human rights treaties discussed in this report. Therefore, the analysis of the human rights violated by restrictive abortion laws and criminal procedure in Chile set out in this report includes both an examination of the applicable domestic and international legal norms.

B.1 THE RIGHT TO FREEDOM FROM DISCRIMINATION BASED ON SOCIAL AND ECONOMIC STATUS

In Chile the selective application of laws on abortion violates the internationally protected right to nondiscrimination for socioeconomic reasons. Article 2 of the Covenant on Economic and Social Rights provides that: "The States Parties to the present Covenant undertake to guarantee that the rights enunciated in the present Covenant will be exercised without discrimination of any kind as to race, colour, sex, language, religion, political or other opinion, national or social origin, property, birth or other status." Article 2 of the Covenant on Civil and Political Rights has a similar provision. One of the fundamental principles of human rights law is that no human right guaranteed in international human rights instruments can be violated because of an individual's economic status.

While well-off women have the economic means to pay for an abortion in a private clinic with expert doctors, poor women often have to undergo high-risk procedures at the hands of untrained persons. If these women suffer complications as a result of such procedures, they must seek medical help at public hospitals. These institutions frequently report them to the police. This situation in itself is a violation of the human rights of the victims of such procedures.

B.2 THE RIGHT TO LIFE, LIBERTY, AND SECURITY

The right to life, liberty, and security is protected by international human rights treaties as well as by the Chilean Constitution. The Universal Declaration states that "all individuals have the right to life, freedom, and personal security."[27] This right is also enumerated in the Covenant on Civil and Political Rights,[28] the Convention of Belém do Pará[29] and the American Convention on Human Rights.[30] At the national level, "the [Chilean] Constitution protects the right to life and the physical and psychological integrity of all persons."[31]

The right to life

The right to life is violated in cases of deaths from pregnancies or childbirth when the pregnancy resulted from the state's failure to guarantee access to basic reproductive health services. Moreover, there is also a violation of the right to life when a law such as Chile's abortion law does not allow women access to certain reproductive health services.[32]

Article 6.1 of the Covenant on Civil and Political Rights establishes that "the right to life is inherent to the human person. This right is protected by law. No one may be arbitrarily deprived of life. "While this provision has traditionally been applied only to due process in cases of the applicability of the death penalty, the Human Rights Committee recently recommended that state parties to the Covenant more fully implement this article, adopting positive measures to ensure its protection.[33] Moreover, in its recommendations to Peru on November 6, 1996, the Human Rights Committee stated with respect to Peru's abortion law: "The Committee is also concerned that abortion gives rise to a criminal penalty even if a woman is pregnant as a result of rape and that clandestine abortions are the main cause of maternal mortality. These provisions not only mean that women are subject to inhumane treatment but are possibly incompatible with articles 3, 6, and 7 of the Covenant."[34] The Committee specifically recommends that Peru "take the necessary measures to ensure that women do not risk their life because of the existence of restrictive legal provisions on abortion."[35]

Article 19 of the Chilean Constitution assures all persons "the right to life and to physical and psychological integrity." In Chile the absolute prohibition on abortion violates this right to life. Women whose life is threatened by pregnancy are prohibited from having an abortion that would save their life. Furthermore, low-income women who are forced by their social or economic circumstances to have an abortion must resort to unsanitary procedures that put their lives at risk.

The above argument is supported by statistics that reveal the danger of clandestine abortion. Specialized studies demonstrate that legal abortion has a mortality rate of less than one for every 100,000 procedures,[36] while clandestine abortion in Latin America is estimated to cause the death of 50 to 100 women for every 100,000 procedures.[37] It is estimated that 70,000 women every year die from clandestine and unsafe abortions worldwide.[38] These figures demonstrate that the fact that it is illegal for health services to provide abortions threatens women's life and health.

The criminalization of abortion does not reduce its incidence but instead converts it into a clandestine procedure.[39] The proportion of pregnancies that result in abortions is larger in Latin America than in any other region of the world, in spite of the fact that abortion is illegal in all countries except for Cuba, Guyana, and Barbados.[40] Of the six countries studied in a 1994 report (Brazil, Colombia, Chile, Mexico, Peru, and the Dominican Republic), Chile had the highest proportion of abortion.[41] It is estimated that in Chile one of every three pregnancies ends in abortion,[42] compared with 9% of pregnancies that end in abortion in The Netherlands, 17% in France, and 30% in the United States, countries where abortion is legal and accessible.[43]

The right to liberty and security

According to international human rights laws, states cannot force women to conceive a child against their will. The Covenant on Civil and Political Rights, as well as the American Convention on Human Rights, establish that "every one has the right to liberty and security of person. No one shall be deprived of his liberty except on such grounds and in accordance with such procedures as are established by law...."[44] The decision to have a child should be "a voluntary and autonomous one, and a positive and enriching experience for the woman. To prevent this from occurring by forcing a woman to carry an undesired pregnancy to term and to deal with the consequences is to compromise her freedom, dignity, and right to decide, and to condemn her to a future she did not choose."[45] As the Cairo Programme of Action affirms, states have "first and foremost" the "obligation" to "ensure that every child born is a wanted child."[46] The state that prohibits abortion and fails to offer adequate access to contraceptive methods leaves women at risk of unwanted pregnancies, thus endangering their health and autonomy. Another example that compromises women's autonomy and security is when women are harassed, subjected to ignominious trials, and put in jail for having an abortion, as were many of the women in this report.

B.3 THE RIGHT TO FREEDOM FROM DISCRIMINATION ON THE BASIS OF GENDER

The right to be free from discrimination on the basis of gender is one of the cornerstones of human rights under international law.[47] The Women's Convention requires all states parties to "repeal all penal provisions which constitute discrimination against women."[48]

Abortion laws, as well as their discriminatory application against the poorest women, perpetuate a paternalistic control over women's reproductive lives, and constitute a form of discrimination on the basis of gender. The prosecution of women who have had abortions violates the rights of women who are pregnant against their will.[49] The Chilean state has committed itself to guaranteeing the rights protected by the Women's Convention, "by ... eliminating discrimination against women."[50] For example, women's right to health, protected by Article 12 of the Women's Convention and Article 12 of the Covenant on Economic and Social Rights, among other treaties, is violated when the law prohibits a medical procedure that is practiced exclusively on women. In fact, all the violations of rights discussed in this chapter can also be characterized as violations to the right of nondiscrimination on the basis of gender.

B.4 THE RIGHT TO HEALTH, REPRODUCTIVE HEALTH, AND FAMILY PLANNING

Both international human rights treaties and Chile's Constitution guarantee the rights to health, reproductive health, and family planning.

The right to health

The right to health is recognized in the Universal Declaration[51] as well as in the Covenant on Economic and Social Rights, which provides that: "[t]he States Parties to the present Covenant recognize the right of everyone to the enjoyment of the highest attainable standard of physical and mental health."[52] Moreover, "the Chilean Constitution ensures to all persons the right to health. The state protects the free and equal access of all to protection and recuperation of one's health and to rehabilitative measures."[53] The Women's Convention, which will be discussed in the following section, also compels the states parties to protect women's right to health.

When the state does not permit abortion, and pregnancy results in health problems or even in death (whether from a clandestine abortion or from childbirth complications), women are denied the right to medical attention and health guaranteed by the Constitution and international treaties. Furthermore, the possibility of being arrested and prosecuted can deter women who have undergone clandestine abortions from seeking medical attention when complications occur.

The right to reproductive health and family planning

Three different provisions of the Women's Convention incorporate reproductive health and family planning as components of the right to health. Article 12 establishes that "the States Parties shall take all appropriate measures to eliminate discrimination against women in the field of health care in order to ensure, on a basis of equality of men and women, access to health care services, including those related to family planning."[54] The Convention also states that "States Parties shall take all appropriate measures to ... ensure [women in rural areas] ... the right ... (b) to have access to adequate health care facilities, including information, counseling, and services in family planning."[55] With regard to family planning, the Convention establishes that "States Parties ... shall ensure, on a basis of equality of men and women ... (e)the same rights to decide freely and responsibly on the number and spacing of their children and to have access to the information, education, and means to enable them to exercise these rights...."[56]

In establishing these rights for women, the Women's Convention goes beyond the right to health, and compels states parties, including Chile, to offer adequate family planning services. The Cairo Programme of Action and the Beijing Platform consider abortion in dangerous conditions a grave public health problem that puts the lives of a large number of women at risk.[57] These documents also ask states to give "accurate" information and "comprehensive counseling" to all women who have unwanted pregnancies and, as stated by one commentator, to "ensure that women who have suffered complications following an abortion have timely access to health services, counseling, and post-abortion education in order to avoid finding themselves in the same situation again."[58] The treatment of Chilean women who go to public hospitals for help reveals a very different reality. Of course, it is important to underscore that even if there were adequate family planning services, there still would be unwanted pregnancies.[59]

B.5 THE RIGHT TO PRIVACY

The Covenant on Civil and Political Rights states that "no one shall be subjected to arbitrary or unlawful interference with his privacy, family, home, or correspondence, nor to unlawful attacks on his honour or reputation."[60] The Chilean Constitution also ensures "respect and protection for one's private and public life and the dignity of the person and his family...."[61] More specifically, the Ethics Code of the Chilean Medical Association provides that confidentiality between doctor and patient is a right as well as a duty of the professional, even when the patient is not under his or her care.

As this report demonstrates (see the section on "Reporting of the Crime"), most of the cases where women were reported to the police for abortion occurred when a medical professional reported a woman to the police after she gave the professional information on her condition for the purpose of obtaining medical treatment. This behavior on the part of medical professionals violates the rights of these women to privacy and patient confidentiality.

B.6 THE RIGHT TO LEGAL ASSISTANCE

Article 14(3)(d) of the Covenant on Civil and Political Rights establishes the obligation of states to provide legal assistance to those who do not have the means to pay for it. The same principle is also found in Article 8 related to one's rights at trial in the American Convention on Human Rights.[62] Article 19 (3) of the 1980 Chilean Constitution establishes "the equal protection of the law in the exercise of one's rights. Every person has the right to legal assistance in the manner established by law, and no authority or individual can impede, restrict, or undermine the lawful intervention of a person's lawyer unless the law so requires.... The law shall provide for the means to ensure legal assistance and defense counsel to those who cannot obtain it for themselves."

This report shows that many women prosecuted for abortion in Chile lack legal representation. (See the section below, "Right to Defense"). On average, only 38% of the accused women had access to defense counsel, and 60% had no legal assistance. When a lawyer participated in the defense, it was primarily in those cases where the accused was imprisoned. The defense is dispensed with voluntarily or by force for lack of resources when there is no detention. Although the petition to suspend imprisonment does not legally require the intervention of a lawyer, a lawyer is in fact necessary when a person, particularly a woman with no criminal record, is imprisoned before trial without legal justification. Adequate assistance from defense counsel is vital to securing release on bail or provisional release prior to trial. The lack of legal assistance provided to women prosecuted for abortion shows that within the context of abortion prosecutions, there are clear violations of international treaties to which Chile is a party, as well as of human rights protected by the Chilean Constitution.

B.7 THE RIGHT TO DUE PROCESS AND TO BE PRESUMED INNOCENT

In addition to violating the right to legal assistance, prosecutions of women who have abortions violate other rights as a result of their being subjected to preventive, or pretrial, imprisonment.[63] The Covenant on Civil and Political Rights provides that preventive imprisonment prior to trial should not be the general rule.[64] The American Convention on Human Rights holds that "[e]very person accused of a criminal offense has the right to be presumed innocent so long as his guilt has not been proven according to law...."[65] Article 19(7)(e) of the Chilean Constitution provides that preventive imprisonment should be considered only when the judge finds it necessary under the Criminal Procedure Code.[66]

In Chile, judicial practice demonstrates that preventive imprisonment is the rule rather than the exception. More specifically, as this report shows, preventive imprisonment is used frequently in abortion cases (see the section on "Preventive Imprisonment" below). Fifty-seven percent of women who had abortions spent time in prison. Close to 48% were in prison for less than 14 days, although a woman from Temuco spent almost seven months in prison in 1990. The fact that preventive imprisonment is the rule rather than the exception in Chilean criminal procedure is evident not only from empirical observation but also from judicial practice and the provisions of the Criminal Procedure Code.[67]

As this chapter has shown, Chile, through its laws on abortion, its laws and practice related to criminal procedure, and the behavior of some officials, has violated and continues to violate numerous human rights of women who have obtained abortions and other persons involved in clandestine abortions.

From an interview by the Open Forum on September 25, 1997, in the "Chin Chin" prison facility in Puerto Montt, Chile. On that date, there were 22 women imprisoned there for abortion-related offenses, who were accused of having abortions or providing abortions to other women.

Cristina, 20-years-old and illiterate, got pregnant in the countryside, on one of the Cabuco Islands. When she realized she was pregnant, afraid of her family's reaction and with no support from her boyfriend, she left for the city where she found work in a store. A friend offered to take her to a woman who did abortions very discretely. The woman charged her 30,000 pesos (approximately U.S. $66), which Cristina raised only through great effort. She even borrowed money from her roommate. The method used was a surgical probe. She developed an infection, which gave her a high fever and badly frightened her. The woman who performed the abortion told her to go to the emergency health unit and say she had fallen off the roof of her house and onto a pile of wood. She managed to get to a hospital where they took care of her but they demanded to know who had performed the abortion. No matter how much they threatened her, Cristina remained silent — she remembered the woman had threatened to tell all to the police if her name was revealed. She was so frightened she said nothing and still keeps the woman's name a secret. Her family knows nothing and her friend has been to see her a couple times. She has been in jail for 16 months.

CHAPTER II:
HEALTH POLICY IN CHILE AND ABORTION AS A PUBLIC HEALTH PROBLEM

A. HEALTH POLICY IN CHILE

According to international human rights treaties and other international instruments, the state has certain areas of responsibility it cannot delegate, including health promotion and protection. Nevertheless, the neoliberal economic model that inspired the current Constitution has led to a significant deterioration of the state's capacity to improve on these areas. First, during the 1973–90 military regime, economic resources devoted to health were dramatically reduced. During the last seven years, in spite of the fact that this sector has increasingly become a priority, there seem to be few concrete improvements. The coverage, effectiveness, and quality of health services remains inadequate, and the public health sector focuses on a curative rather than preventive approach in the provision of health services.

The language used in the Constitution reflects the ideological differences between the 1980 Constitution and international treaties that protect the right to health. One of the initial drafts of the constitutional provision on the right to health provided that this right should be guaranteed. The final version specifies that the Constitution "protects free and equal access...." to health services. This modification originated in the Consejo de Estado.[68] Moreover, the courts have concluded that citizens cannot present a request for protection (*recurso de protección*) alleging a state violation of this principle when a private insurance company refuses to pay medical expenses. The courts have held that these cases do not violate the right to health but the right to property, which originates in the contractual relationship, a right that includes incorporating such property interests into the assets of the plaintiff.[69] The protection of the right to health set forth in the Chilean Constitution is only a declaration of principles. It does not ensure the right of everyone to live a dignified life, especially not the poor.[70] As a result women are left unprotected, their human and constitutional rights to physical and psychological integrity are violated. The cases included in this report demonstrate the lack of protection given to women in matters related to their health.

At the policy level, the Maternal and Perinatal Health Program is the

Ministry of Health's principal reproductive heath program both in terms of scope and coverage.[71] The primary activities of this program are related to pregnancy, childbirth, and nursing.[72] Other services include responsible parenthood, defined as the services provided to women or couples of reproductive age (15 – 49) who wish to control fertility; consultations related to sexually transmitted infections; and hospitalization for abortion.[73] This last service is defined as the medical services provided to a woman from the moment she enters an obstetrics and gynecology unit following an abortion procedure or miscarriage.[74]

B. ABORTION IN CHILE: A PUBLIC HEALTH PROBLEM

Public health statistics show that the number of women hospitalized for abortion complications has remained more or less constant. Between 1983 and 1984 there were 42,000 cases, while between 1990 and 1991 the figure increased to 44,000.[75] Seventy-five percent of such cases are induced abortions, as opposed to miscarriages. Health authorities and others estimate that only 25% of the women who have abortions suffer complications. Nevertheless, in spite of a slow decline in numbers beginning in 1964 to the present, (see Bar Graph 2), abortion is still the leading cause of maternal mortality in Chile. Close to a third of maternal deaths are estimated to be directly related to abortion; furthermore, it is believed that this figure is lower than the actual figure. A 1984 study based on death certificates determined with certainty that out of 59 maternal deaths following abortions, four corresponded to spontaneous abortions (miscarriages) and 24 to induced abortions. The rest could not be determined with exactitude, although the study concluded that they were deaths from induced abortions, based on the characteristics, circumstances, and complications of the cases.[76]

Bar Graph 2: Number of Maternal Mortalities

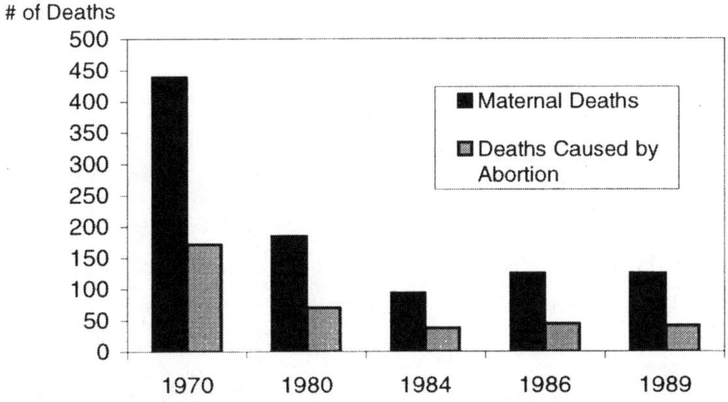

Source: APROFA Bulletin, Year XVIII, 1992, and APROFA Records 1991, 1991

Obstetric expenditures in 1991 represented between 25% and 30% of all health service expenditures. In some hospitals in the Santiago metropolitan region, however, this figure reached almost 52%.

Abortion, when performed under adequate medical conditions, is unlikely to have any negative impact on women's health.[77] During the 1970s and 1980s, there was a decrease in the maternal mortality and morbidity rates of the procedure in those countries where abortion was legalized. However, because of abortion's illegal status, the tens of thousands of abortions practiced every year in Chile must be practiced clandestinely. This fact, together with the poverty of most women who seek abortions, constitutes an invitation to unqualified people to perform unsanitary and unsafe abortions. Frequently the pregnant woman induces her own abortion, using ancient and well-known techniques such as the insertion of wires, sticks, and/or toothpicks into the vagina. In other cases, women seek help from third parties who have had experience in these procedures.

Abortion procedures used by pregnant women or by a midwife with no training, and where sanitary conditions are lacking, can cause multiple complications that range from slight to severe. The damage can include "chronic inflammation, sterility, menstrual alterations, pregnancy and childbirth complications in future births, and possible rupture of internal scars from previous perforations caused by abortions."[78] Some experts believe that there is also psychological trauma resulting from abortion, although others disagree, arguing there is only a sort of post-abortion relief.[79] Another grave complication of abortion is sterility caused by perforation of the genital organs or by a widespread genital infection. Among the women in this study, seven (4.5%) had their reproductive organs removed, in most cases a total hysterectomy. Sometimes other complications were accompanied by peritonitis. Two of the women suffered a tear in their intestine which resulted in a colonectomy, one of them in Santiago (1991) and the other in Arica (1983). A study done at Salvador Hospital in Santiago showed that out of 84 patients with secondary infertility, at least 6% had had at least one induced abortion. Eleven of the 21 hysterectomies performed in that hospital's gynecological unit, more than 50%, were the consequence of an abortion.[80]

The methods used to induce abortion by the women studied were high-risk methods (see Chart 3). The surgeon's probe was the most-used method (61%). Depending on the midwife's skill, this is a sterile probe whose application may be accompanied by injectable antibiotics. It was more commonly used in Santiago. In Santiago, 8% of the pregnancies were interrupted by curettage (scraping the uterus), in most cases by a paramedic using medical instruments. The introduction of sticks and plant stems at home represented 8% of induced abortions, followed by vaginal douches. The introduction of toothpicks and wires in the vagina is an extremely high-risk practice because they might perforate the walls of the uterus.

Chart 3: Types of Abortion Procedures for All Cities

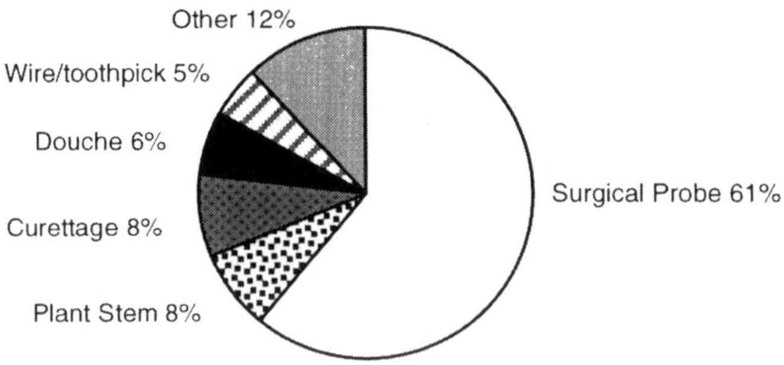

There is also evidence of the use of injectable drugs intended to provoke dilation or contractions in order to induce an abortion. Together with other commonly used drugs, such as quinine, such drugs can have serious side effects.[81] For example, there can be allergic reactions, some highly toxic, causing death by kidney or respiratory collapse, among others.[82]

From an interview by the Open Forum on September 25, 1997, in the "Chin Chin" prison facility in Puerto Montt, Chile. On that date, there were 22 women imprisoned there for abortion-related offenses, who were accused of having abortions or providing abortions to other women.

Sandra, 24-years-old, a prostitute, says that she got pregnant by accident, without knowing who the father was. Alone and without any money to survive during her pregnancy, she decided to have an abortion, which seemed free of complications. But since she had to continue working, she did not get the rest she needed, much less the medical care, so one day while working she suddenly began to hemorrhage. She ended up in the emergency room where she states that she was mistreated. After her release from the hospital, she was taken directly to jail.

CHAPTER III: ANALYSIS OF DOMESTIC LEGISLATION AND COURT RECORDS: WOMEN PROSECUTED FOR ABORTION

A. THE LEGAL FRAMEWORK OF ABORTION IN CHILE

In Chile, abortion is illegal under any circumstance. Abortion is prohibited by the Criminal Code, articles 342 to 245. It is classified under "Crimes against the Family Order and Public Morality." The Chilean law on abortion is one of the most restrictive in the world. The Chilean Criminal Code, which dates back to 1896, is the oldest in Latin America. Its framework for penalizing abortion is derived from the 1850 Spanish Criminal Code,[83] whose provisions related to abortion have been completely reformed in modern Spain. The Chilean Criminal Code does not define abortion, but in 1963 a Supreme Court ruling defined it as the malicious interruption of pregnancy for the purpose of avoiding the birth of a fetus or of interrupting the natural course of pregnancy. The Criminal Code punishes every kind of intentional abortion, as well as abortions caused by an intentional or unintentional violent act on a woman whose pregnancy is evident. The law punishes both the woman who consents to having an abortion and the abortion provider. The statutory punishment for abortion is three to five years of imprisonment for obtaining an abortion and 541 days to three years for providing one, with medical professionals involved in abortions receiving more severe penalties.

In spite of the restrictive provisions of the Criminal Code, therapeutic abortion was permitted by the Health Code from 1931 to 1989. During this period, women whose lives were in danger could obtain an abortion with the approval of two doctors. In 1989, during the last weeks of Pinochet's military dictatorship, therapeutic abortion was eliminated. The draftors of the 1989 law concluded that "considering the advances in modern medicine, therapeutic abortion is not justified under any circumstance."[84]

By abolishing therapeutic abortion, Chilean criminal law subordinates a woman and her life to the life of the fetus. This position is reinforced by the 1980 Constitution, which protects the lives of "the unborn" in the same article as other basic rights. Thus, the life of the fetus is considered to be separate from the pregnant woman's right to choose whether to continue the pregnancy. Furthermore, all institutional mechanisms available, including the police, are used to "protect" the life of the fetus.[85]

Following the logic of Chilean law, although the right to life is guaranteed by the Constitution, women's right to life is subordinated to their obligation to carry to term all pregnancies, even those that are unwanted, including those that result from contraceptive failure, from ignorance of correct contraceptive use, from rape, and even when the pregnancy endangers a woman's life. Thus, under Chilean law, women's lives and bodies are nothing more than a vessel, and it is the state, not women, that has control over women's bodies.

In spite of this, women still have abortions as the last recourse against an unwanted pregnancy. Of all the cases of abortion penalized by Chilean criminal law, the types of abortions that are predominant in this report are self-induced (Article 344) or those performed on them with their consent (Article 342 (3)).

B. PARTICIPATION IN AND CRIMINAL RESPONSIBILITY FOR ABORTION

In Chilean law there are three types of participation in a crime that determine responsibility for such crime: principal, accomplice, and accessory. The principal is the main person responsible for a crime, the person who had control over the criminal action, that is, the person who both objectively and subjectively controlled the criminal behavior, in such a way that he or she was the person who decided to consummate the crime.[86] Accomplices are those who, not being the principal, cooperate with the criminal behavior before or during its commission.[87] Accessories are those who, not having participated in the crime, but knowing a crime to already have been committed by another, aid the principal in some way, such as by receiving, hiding or supplying the means or instruments to avoid capture.[88]

Other terms used in this report include women who have had abortions and abortion providers, also referred to as midwives in other studies. Abortion providers are the third parties who perform an abortion procedure on a pregnant woman with her consent.[89]

B.1 ANALYSIS OF THE OFFENDERS BY GENDER

Court records show that most of the persons found guilty of abortion were women. Table 4 shows that, between 1983 and 1991, men's participation varied between 11% and 20%. The greatest percentages of men convicted of abortion were 29% in 1987 and 21% in 1991.

Table 4: Number of Cases by Type of Responsibility of Those Convicted

	1983	1984	1985	1986	1987	1988	1989	1991
Type of Responsibility								
Principal	98	93	92	61	91	83	55	32
Women	86	85	78	55	66	68	46	24
Men	12	8	14	6	25	15	9	8
Accomplice	10	4	7	10	6	6	3	6
Women	3	1	5	7	5	5	2	5
Men	7	3	2	3	1	1	1	1
Accessory	1	1	---	1	7	2	3	---
Women	---	1	---	1	3	1	1	---
Men	1	---	---	---	4	1	2	---
Total	109	98	99	72	104	91	61	38
Women	89	87	83	63	74	74	49	29
Men	20	11	16	9	30	17	12	9

Source: Justice Yearbooks 1983, 1984, 1985, 1986, 1987, 1988, 1989, and 1991 published by the National Statistics Institute. The figures for 1990 are not available.

Table 5 shows participation in the cases studied according to sex. It differentiates between principal-participant, the principals who obtained abortions, and principal-providers. This distinction derives from the courts, which have held that a principal-participant need not have taken part directly in the abortion procedure, but is still a principal of the crime because he or she either supplied the means to carry out the procedure or observed the procedure without taking part in it. The total number of those involved in this study, whether as principals of the abortion, providers, or accomplices was 221; of these, 159 were women who had an abortion. Of these 159, four were minor women who reported having had an abortion performed on them without their consent (victims of abortion). The others were women who had an abortion with their consent; of these, 145 were adults of majority age and 10 were minors; five of the minors were indicted and five were not. The total sum of persons involved also includes 39 coprincipals or providers, eight principal-participants, and 15 accomplices. The total number of women involved was 200 (90%), compared with 21 men (10%).

Table 5: Participation and Gender of the Defendants

	Women	Men	Total	%
Participation				
Women who had abortions-principal	155	--	155	70%
Victims of Abortion (no consent)	4	--	4	2%
Co-principals	31	8	39	18%
Principal-participant	4	4	8	4%
Accomplice or Accessory	6	9	15	7%
Total	200	21	221	100%*

*The percentages are approximate and may not add up to 100%.

Women's participation in abortion varies from year to year in the research undertaken and from city to city. Chart 6 shows the distribution by year of women's participation in the cases studied. The analysis consistently shows that each year women undergo criminal prosecution mostly for having induced their own abortion. The percentage of women tried as coprincipals fluctuated between 26% and 20% (1983 and 1990) and 10% and 11% (1984 and 1991).

Chart 6: Women's Participation in Abortion

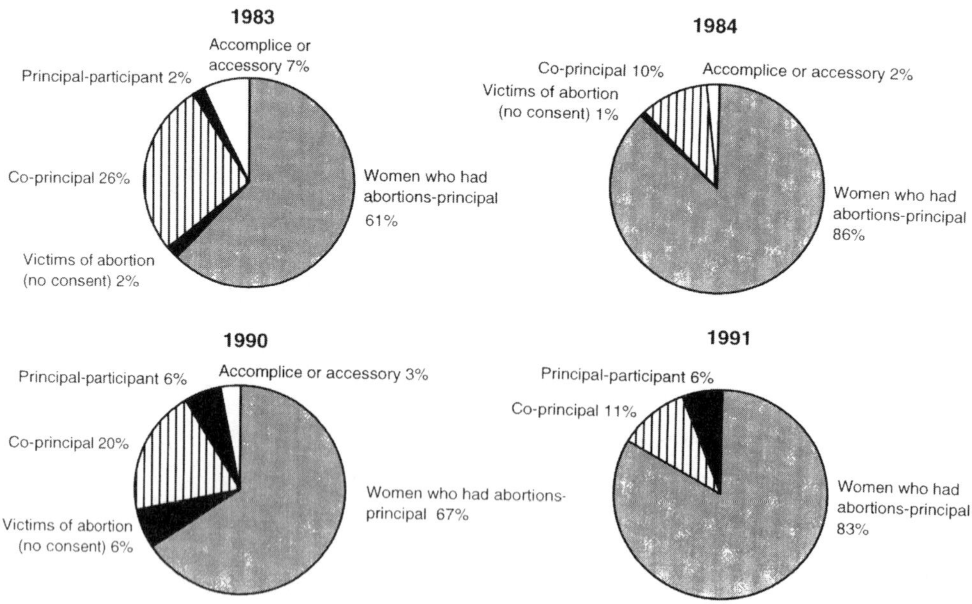

*The percentages are approximate and may not add up to 100%.

B.2 NUMBER OF CASES BY CITY

The cases included in this report cover four Chilean cities, although most of them are from Santiago, followed by Valparaiso, Arica, and Temuco, in that order. The intake of abortion cases countrywide show the same order of prevalence. The National Statistics Institute has statistics on new abortion cases filed every year, according to information provided by the courts (see table 7).[90]

Table 7: Incoming Cases by Court of Appeals

	Santiago	Valparaíso	Arica	Temuco	Total
1983	120	74	6	31	231
1984	197	60	10	17	284
1991	45	38	1	13	97
Total	362	172	17	61	612

Source: National Statistics Institute

Table 8 breaks down the cases reviewed in this report by year and territory. The number of cases identified is clearly larger than the number of cases reviewed. The difference between the number of cases identified and the number of cases reviewed — see tables 7 and 8 — resulted from the impossibility of locating all court records. In Santiago it was possible to review 90 cases; in Valparaiso, 32; in Arica, 18; and in Temuco, 13. The greatest number of cases was filed in 1984, according to the records of incoming cases in these areas, although NSI figures show 1984 as having the second-highest number of cases filed nationally. A countrywide NSI statistics summary shows that there were 605 incoming cases in 1983; 503 in 1984; 258 in 1990; and 230 in 1991.

Table 8: Incoming Cases by Court of Appeals

	Santiago	Valparaíso	Arica	Temuco	Total
1983	15	6	4	6	31
1984	62	9	10	2	83
1990	8	8	3	3	22
1991	5	9	1	2	17
Total	90	32	18	13	153

Other figures collected by the NSI show new data on the number of people arrested for abortion. The Intelligence Police (*Policía de Investigaciones*) maintain a record of people arrested and referred to the courts according to the crime. Bar Graph 9 shows the number of persons arrested for abortion from Intelligence Police records, and not the number of cases being prosecuted.[91]

Bar Graph 9: People Arrested and Referred to Courts for Abortion, by City

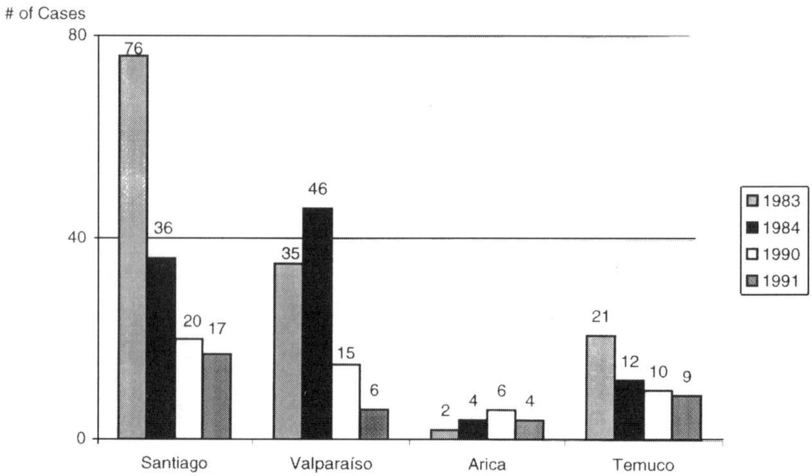

Source: Police Statistics Yearbooks, 1983, 1984, 1990, and 1991, National Statistic Institute and Intelligence Police (*Policía de Investigaciones*), published in separate years, National Statistics Institute, Santiago.

The largest number of persons referred to the courts by the police for abortions was in 1983, the year that, according to court statistics, had the highest number of incoming cases. The only difference between these two sources was in Valparaiso, where the figure was 35 arrested and referred to courts in 1983, compared with 46 in 1984.

C. THE CRIMINAL PROCESS IN CHILE

C.1 THE REPORTING OF THE CRIME

In contrast to the Anglo-American adversarial justice system, in Chile, a civil law country, the courts, composed of one or more judges, both investigate and determine the guilt or innocence of the accused; in order to initiate the criminal process, the court must be informed of the crime. This information can reach the court by various means depending on the category of crime or misdemeanor, since some kinds of crimes require a complaint from the injured party and some do not. According to the Criminal Procedure Code, the criminal process can be initiated either by a reporting of the crime, a complaint, a petition by the Attorney General's Office (*Ministerio Público*), or because the judge investigating one crime has sufficient cause to initiate an investigation into another crime.[92] Any person can report a crime without being part of the criminal process.[93] Crimes can be reported to the courts, to the police (*Carabineros*) or to the Intelligence Police (*Policía de Investigación*). Table 10 shows that all of the prosecutions for abortion reviewed were initiated by a report, usually from someone affiliated with an institution.

Table 10: Reports Against Women Who Had Abortions, Classified by Origin of the Report

	Total 1983-84; 1990-91	
Institutional	**#**	**%**
Hospital	127	80%
Police *(Carabineros)*	7	4%
Intelligence Police	3	2%
Other	1	1%
Sub-total	138	87%
Non-Institutional	**#**	**%**
Partner (boyfriend/husband)	8	5%
Family member	9	6%
Stranger	1	1%
Herself	3	2%
Sub-total	21	14%
Total	**159**	**100%***

*Approximate figures

Institutional reporting on patient confidentiality: The legal framework

Health professionals have an obligation to protect patient confidentiality and to respect a patient's privacy, an obligation that derives both from ethical obligations and the Constitution. Article 19 of the Constitution creates this obligation in its fourth clause, which guarantees "respect and protection for the private and public life of an individual and his or her reputation and that of his or her family."[94] Article 10 of the Chilean Medical Professional Association also establishes that patient confidentiality is a physician's right and duty, even when the patient is not under his or her care.

In order to enforce and provide content for this constitutional norm, criminal law classifies as "slander and insult" the undertaking of a public or private act intended to damage a person's reputation. The Criminal Code also protects client and patient confidentiality: it is a crime to reveal information gained through a professional relationship with a client or patient. Article 247 (2) of the Criminal Code makes it a criminal offense for anyone who "in the exercise of any profession that requires a degree, reveals the secrets entrusted to him or her by reason of that profession."[95]

Furthermore, the Criminal Procedure Code specifically exonerates professionals from making statements at trial or providing information for a criminal investigation if it means the breach of patient or client confidentiality. Article 201(2) provides that the following persons do not have the obligation to provide statements in criminal trials or investigations: "those who, because of their status, profession or legal function, such as a lawyer, doctor, or priest, have the duty to keep the secret entrusted to them, but only with respect to information directly related to this secret."[96]

Article 84 (5) of the Criminal Procedure Code provides that the following persons do have the obligation to report crimes: "the directors of hospital facilities or private clinics and, generally, medical, dental, chemical, and pharmaceutical professionals as well as professionals from other disciplines related to health preservation and restoration, and the professional support staff of these disciplines, when they find in a person or corpse indications of a crime or a misdemeanor."[97] Article 494 (9) of the Criminal Procedure Code classifies as an offense the failure to report a crime in accordance with the previous provision, stating that "the physician who, finding in a person or corpse signs of poisoning or any other serious crime, does not report it to the authorities in a timely manner" is guilty of a criminal offense.[98] Frequently these two articles are cited as creating the obligation to report or a justification for reporting abortion, an interpretation that only some doctors and lawyers agree on.[99]

According to Alfredo Etcheberry,[100] the Chilean legal system establishes an absolute protection of client and patient confidentiality, and the only exception is article 20 of the Health Code. This article compels physicians to report contagious diseases listed in the regulations.[101] According to this legal scholar, there is no obligation to report an abortion, since it is not a contagious disease. Moreover, this argument is supported by the exculpatory nature of fulfilling one's duty to maintain confidentiality under Article 10 (10) of the Criminal Code. Likewise article 20 (2) of the Criminal Procedure Code exempts professionals from making statements in criminal proceedings in order to protect patient and client confidentiality. Etcheberry asserts that respecting these provisions is the correct interpretation of articles 84 (5) of the Criminal Procedure Code and article 494 (9) of the Criminal Code.[102]

On the other hand, there are criminal law scholars in Chile who hold that in spite of patient confidentiality, there are certain cases in which a professional should reveal the secret entrusted to him or her. For example, confidential information can be revealed when the affected party consents to it, or when the law permits it. Eduardo Novoa Monreal[103] holds that public interest justifies the breach of patient confidentiality, as in the cases of articles 84 and 494 of the Criminal Procedure Code previously quoted.

The right to keep a private clinic's medical records secret was defended successfully in a recent case before the Chilean Supreme Court, a ruling that was based on the right to patient confidentiality.[104] Two physicians from Victoria, near Temuco, were tried for the crime established in article 494 (9) of the Criminal Procedure Code. This criminal prosecution was initiated in 1984 against two physicians who saw Maria Eugenia, one of the women included in the present research. The doctors said that even though a midwife said that the abortion had been induced, from a medical point of view they could not determine whether it was induced or spontaneous, so they did not report it. Nevertheless, the trial judge said in his ruling that they "... had the obligation to report the incident to the authorities, who are the ones who must decide what the facts were." The Supreme Court reversed this ruling on appeal.

Institutional reporting

In this study, institutional reporting of abortion refers to reports made by hospitals, the police, or other institutions, or by individuals acting on behalf of an institution or because they are affiliated with an institution.

Notwithstanding the controversy surrounding the duty to report a crime and the protection of patient confidentiality, the fact remains that, as is apparent in Table 10, the percentage of institutional reports is about 87%. Of all the cases reviewed, only one person turned herself in for abortion, a midwife whose patient died after the procedure.

The highest number of institutional reports came from the public hospitals where women sought help. Ninety-two percent of institutional reports came from hospitals, and 80% of all reports were made by hospitals. All the hospitals that reported women for abortion were public; there was no instance of a private hospital or clinic reporting an abortion to the police.

Each institution and its staff has a specific procedure for reporting abortions. Most do so with a telephone call or in person to a police officer assigned to the hospital. Court records show that some hospitals, such as Felix Bulnes Hospital which is part of the Western Santiago Metropolitan Health Services, had, at least during the 1983–1984 period, the policy of reporting women for abortion through certain pre-established formalities: the Chief of Services sent the Hospital Director a list of the women admitted to maternity services with a diagnosis of induced abortion. The Hospital Director then sent the list to the Director of the Western Santiago Metropolitan Health Services, who then remitted the list to the Institution's Legal Department, which then reported the women on the list.

This system is illustrated by Felix Bulnes Hospital's internal memo No. 71, written in March 1984, which provides as follows: "Please find attached the list of patients admitted to the isolation sections for induced abortion in February." This list of patients includes the names and addresses of 17 women. Some of these reports included the patient's medical record, including her "confession" and the means used for abortion: "probe," "parsley," etc. Also included on the list were those women who had not "confessed," and on their file was written: "woman denies abortion procedure."

The reports of the Legal Department of the Metropolitan Health Services read as follows: " … who on June the 8th, 1984, asks for an investigation to be opened against M.A. for the possible crime of abortion, that a file be opened and that she be punished with the highest penalty for this crime…." Two things are remarkable in this formal claim for prosecution and punishment. First, in spite of the fact that only a possible abortion is being reported, the letter asks for the highest penalty to be applied. Second, the report is presented by health care professionals, whose duty is to protect patient confidentiality.

Moreover, in addition to this formal report, other officials at the Felix

Bulnes Hospital used more efficient methods of reporting abortions. Midwives or physicians called the policeman on duty in the hospital to arrest and question the patient. Sometimes the patient was arrested as soon as she was admitted to the hospital, and interrogated while she received medical attention. A policeman's statement, found in court records, explains the process:

> "He was doing the second round of his shift at the Children's Emergency Room in the Felix Bulnes Hospital, when around 0:30 the Midwife told him that [the woman] had induced her own abortion, and that I should take the necessary measures. I immediately sent notice to the Walker Martínez Sub-station and kept the suspect, S.V.B.V., under arrest. During the interrogation she kept silent and refused to say if there was a third party involved." (Santiago, 1984)

A physician, M.B., a public employee of the Juan de Noé Hospital in Arica questioned patients like a policeman, not a health care professional who has sworn to care for his patients and protect patient confidentiality. In 1983 and 1984, two women admitted to this hospital were forced to sign "confessions" dictated by the physician and written down by a midwife. One of the women declared at trial that she signed the paper because "the doctor wouldn't take care of her otherwise." The other woman said the doctor had threatened to withhold authorization for release from the hospital if she did not sign. In both cases the signed "confession" was turned over to the police. In the research conducted for this report, it was confirmed that other physicians also showed willingness to punish women who had had abortions. In one medical record the following was recorded:

> Gladys was three months pregnant, working to feed her three children and her husband, who had been banished to the south of the country. Her medical record had the following words in her physician's handwriting: "Must be reported." (Santiago, 1984).

The fear of being reported can be life-threatening. Its consequences range from a dangerous delay in going to a hospital, to flight, to suicide.

> A Valparaiso woman reached the hospital with symptoms of an abortion. While she waited to be admitted, she overheard the

> staff talk about reporting her, and she fled. However, her condition got worse, and she was forced to return. (Valparaiso, 1984.)

In other cases women admitted to public hospitals were frequently very worried about their children left at home alone, and requested to be released before it was prudent to do so.

> Erica was admitted with symptoms of abortion, and ordered rest and medication. She asked to be released as soon as she felt better, arguing that her three children, including a one-and-a-half-year-old girl, needed her. She argued with the physician in charge until she was released under her own responsibility. However, the doctor warned her that if she returned he would not admit her. She returned to her house, where she had a spontaneous abortion. Upon returning to the hospital, the same physician reported her for abortion. (Viña del Mar, 1991)

Women who have abortions, and even the health care staff, describe incidents that closely resemble police interrogations. Women from Arica, Temuco, and Santiago described in their testimonies, both on and off the court records, that before being treated they had to "confess." Flora, from Arica, was warned by the midwives that she would not be taken care of unless she confessed. Emilia, from Temuco, was questioned for two days by the midwives and the physician in charge. The physician declared for the court record:

> "I must add that two days after being admitted the patient investigated admitted in principle *[sic]* that she had induced her abortion, and later she was questioned again and said she had done it herself, introducing an ovulatory *[sic]* pill at home, and later she continued giving false information, saying that it had not been one pill but two, and later she said it had not been with pills but that she had introduced her finger...." (Temuco, 1983)

Statements for the criminal proceedings were also collected while the women were receiving treatment:

> A few minutes before the curettage procedure was started, Lucia was interrogated, but the interrogation had to be suspended because she was going to be operated on. (Santiago 1983)

There are cases in which the health care personnel play a pivotal role in incriminating the woman, arguing vehemently that the abortion was induced:

> The midwife in Ana's case maintained, with all the conviction possible, that the vaginal douche had been used in order to induce an abortion, and even though she couldn't say that the patient had told her so, it was evident, for her, that it was an abortive procedure. (Santiago, 1984)

This same Santiago midwife can frequently be found in court records reporting women. Her signature is in many of the medical records of the women reported, and many of her statements convey this same attitude: the absolute conviction of having observed an induced abortion, without showing judicial officials any doubts. Another midwife, the same one involved in the Felix Bulnes maternity report, was emphatic in her statement against T.S. that her diagnosis of induced abortion was confirmed by the surgical record, which indicated a curettage.

Many women complain in their court statements of being ill-treated by health care personnel. This is not confined to only one hospital: the complaints are common to all the cities included in this research. Marianela, for example, declared before the court that she had had to "confess" her abortion after repeated ill-treatment at the hospital. (Santiago, 1984)

> Luzmenia, seven months pregnant, fell down the stairs while carrying buckets of water. She had to receive urgent medical care from the midwife at the rural clinic. She was ordered bed rest, antispasmodic suppositories, and diazepam. When the symptoms of miscarriage grew worse, she tried to reach the hospital, but it took her husband half an hour to find a horse to go and get help. She gave birth at home. Once she reached the hospital, the doctor ignored her statement. She said, "I wanted that baby, it was my first child and I wanted it. The doctor in Cunco treated me very badly, he said that [sic] [what] things I had put up my vagina, I said nothing. I told him about the fall, but it seems he didn't believe me." Luzmenia was reported for induced abortion. (Temuco, 1984)

When reports are made while the woman who had the abortion is still in the hospital, the criminal process can start with her arrest in the maternity ward. After being released from the hospital, she is immediately taken to the courts to give her statement, opening the file on the case. This occurred in the case of two San Juan de Dios Hospital patients (part of the Western Santiago Metropolitan Health Service) reported by a female physician who called the police requesting their arrest. The poor state of health these women were in when taken to court was recorded, and they were immediately released. The court order reads:

> "...[C]onsidering the merits of this case, and in particular the precarious state of health of the two accused, which is evident to plain sight, and in order to prevent any complications, injury, or illness, they are to be released for lack of merit." (Santiago, 1991)

Reporting by individuals

Close to 13% of the reports in the cases reviewed were presented by individuals who were neither police nor public health services officials (see Table 10). They were presented for the most part by the former partner of the women who had the abortion or by relatives. In many of the cases reviewed, the relatives who reported the abortion were the woman's parents. These two subgroups had different attitudes about the pregnancy and the abortion, as well as different reasons to report their partners or daughters.

The men who reported their partners for abortion were frequently motivated by revenge. In most of the cases, they had broken up on bad terms. These men went to the police without considering the consequences, even when they had taken part in the decision to obtain the abortion or in the abortion procedure itself.

> Viviana worked and supported the family, but her partner was not inclined to work. She was pregnant, and she earned so little as a saleswoman that it was not enough for her and her son, so together she and her partner induced an abortion, using a wire. Soon thereafter she kicked him out of the house for being irresponsible, and he immediately reported her for abortion. (Valparaiso, 1983)

There are different kinds of couples in these cases. Some are married, some cohabit, some are engaged or are just boyfriend and girlfriend.[105] Three boyfriends reported their girlfriends in the cases reviewed.

> Catalina, 15-year-old, was reported by her 17-year-old boyfriend. He accused her mother of forcing her to get an abortion, even though he and his mother were willing to raise the child. Catalina and her mother denied the pregnancy, and held that the boyfriend was angry because Catalina did not want to have sexual relations with him anymore. (Valparaiso, 1990)

There were other instances involving parents. In Arica, a young man accused his partner's mother of forcing her to have an abortion because the mother did not want the child. The couple was living with her mother. Both young people maintained their accusation before the court. In another case, a young woman from Valparaiso was reported by her father, who disliked the man she had relations with. Of the nine relatives who presented reports, seven were mothers who for the most part accused third parties of making the decision or undertaking the procedure.

> Soledad's mother, after hearing her daughter, 19-year-old, describe her abortion, and after taking her to the hospital in very bad shape, went to the boyfriend's workplace — a police station — to report him for forcing her daughter to have an abortion. (Santiago, 1983)

> Rita's mother accused Rita's boyfriend's mother of performing an abortion on Rita, 17-year-old. She filed this report after Rita, who had to be taken to the hospital after suffering complications, told her mother what happened. (Santiago, 1991)

The only other relative who presented a similar report was a woman who reported her sister-in-law while she was in the hospital. The motives that led individuals to report abortions were always related to the pregnancy, romantic relationships, or interpersonal conflicts. These were very complex situations that involved all sorts of emotional and personal issues, making these reports very different from institutional reports.

C.2 THE RIGHT TO LEGAL ASSISTANCE

Chapter I of this report explains how the right to legal assistance is guaranteed by the Chilean Constitution, and by international human rights treaties ratified by Chile. In the cases reviewed, the research undertaken examined the kind of defense counsel the accused had, if any.

The Constitution and international human rights treaties create an obligation that is not being even remotely respected in Chile. The state provides attorneys either through Legal Aid Corporations or public defenders. Legal Aid Corporations are charged with defending those who cannot afford an attorney. They are staffed mostly by candidates for the legal profession, that is, persons who have just completed their law degree and have to work at least six months for one of these institutions in order to qualify as attorneys. These are persons without any experience, who put in few hours a day with the corporation and on average have an excessive workload of 90 to 100 files.

Public defenders are lawyers selected by a judge from a list of non-exempt lawyers. Once a judge selects a lawyer, he or she must defend whomever the judge decides, as long as the defendant does not have his or her own lawyer.[106]

These state-financed institutions simply cannot meet the need for legal assistance and counseling of the poor. In all of the four cities included in this investigation, there are Legal Aid Corporations. There are also other institutions, such as churches and professional associations, that provide legal assistance, but they can reach only a tiny segment of the poor in need of legal services. The result is that the right to legal counsel is moot in most cases, either because there is no one to provide the defense, or because of the bad quality of the service provided.

Chile's inquisitorial criminal procedure system does not allow the defendant's lawyer to intervene in the most important stages of the process, such as the suspect's initial questioning by or statement to police. The law does not require the presence of a lawyer in police interrogations of those suspected of a crime. In the cases reviewed in this report, many of the women gave their first statement while receiving medical attention and were interrogated in the maternity ward, in full view of the medical personnel and the other patients. Although this declaration is not considered dispositive of guilt, it is extremely important, since it can be validated and eventually used to create enough evidence to prosecute and convict the woman. In light of this, it has been proposed that these interrogations, which are usually carried out without a lawyer, be declared null and void.[107]

Two of the women accused of abortion told the court they had been mistreated by the police. One woman stated she had been a victim of illegal coercion by the Intelligence Police; the other woman reported humiliating treatment by the Sexual Crimes Brigade, a specialized division of the same police. Maria Cecilia, one of them, was told to take off her clothes during the interrogation. Then a woman, presumably a policewoman, examined her and told her that she had better tell the truth, because in any case she was still pregnant. She told Maria Cecilia that if she didn't talk, her parents would go to jail (Viña del Mar, 1983). The second case of abuse is narrated by the lawyer of a woman who was admitted to the maternity ward with symptoms of a spontaneous abortion.

> "... she maintains that in the Sexual Crimes Brigade she was treated in a humiliating way, pressured to declare what she had done to herself." The patient had a prolapsed uterus, which might have caused the abortion. (Santiago, 1984)

Defense counsel of women accused of abortion

Court records reviewed for this research show that a significant portion of the women accused of abortion had no defense counsel at all. Bar Graph 11 shows that, of all four cities, the greatest proportion of cases with defense counsel occurred in 1983, with a 64% prevalence. The year with the least prevalence of defense counsel is 1991 — it was provided in only 13% of the cases. On average, only 38% of women included in this study had defense counsel, and 60% had no assistance from a lawyer whatsoever. This is clearly a transgression of the constitutional guarantee of the right to defense counsel, and a violation of the civil and political rights protected by international human rights treaties. These women were not only denied the right to defense counsel but the right to equality before the law.

Bar Graph 11: Representation by Defense Counsel of Women who had Abortions in All Cities

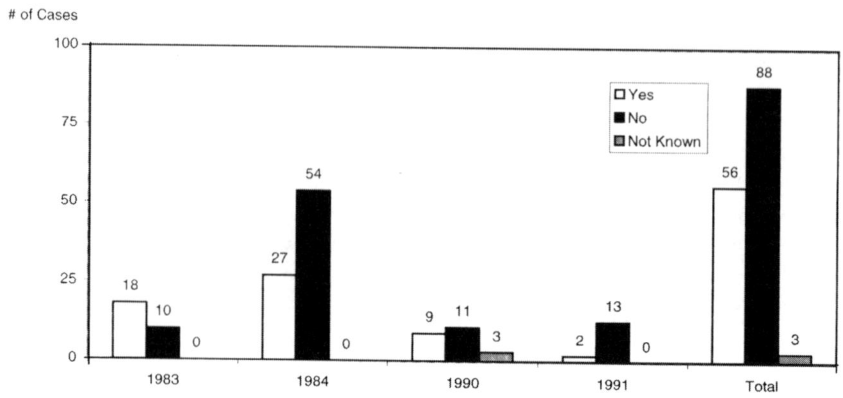

In the cases reviewed, those women who did have an attorney obtained assistance through the Legal Aid Corporation, which provided lawyers to 34 of the 56 women who had legal defense, or 61%. Three women, 5% of the total number, had a lawyer assigned by a judge as a public defender. There is no information for the rest of the cases.

It is clearly important to have legal defense throughout the criminal process, but the quality of the defense is equally important. In two of the cases reviewed, the effort made by the defense attorney was insignificant. The lawyer, assigned by the court, rebutted the accusation in less than a paragraph. Legally, in the rebuttal of the accusation the defense lawyer has the critical opportunity to present the defendant's version of the facts of the case and circumstances, as well as special considerations that merit the defendant's acquittal or attenuates her guilt. Nidia's attorney, however, simply stated:

> "Since N.V. has been accused as the principal in the crime of abortion established in article 342 N.3 (sic) of the Criminal Code, I ask the court to acquit the defendant, since according to her own statements: 'E.A., the Twin, made me have an abortion. I didn't want to go, I wanted to have my child, and they said it was just an injection to check if I was pregnant.' These statements are important in the process, because they show that the accused, N.V., did not have the intention to commit the crime, which was induced by E.A., a.k.a. the Twin, as a way of resolving the prob-

> lem of a third party, the person who caused the pregnancy. For the aforementioned reasons, I ask the court to acquit Mrs. N.V."
>
> THEREFORE: I REQUEST the court to disregard the accusation and acquit Mrs. N.V. (Arica, 1984)

This defense attorney not only did not adequately explain the facts, he also gave up the opportunity to demand a further investigation and to present evidence, and failed to call as a witness the man who got Nidia pregnant and then deceived her. This woman had two different attorneys. The first one was charged with obtaining her release from prison, and the second, named by a judge, was charged with answering the accusation.

Defense counsel of abortion providers, principal-participants and accomplices

Bar Graph 12 shows the frequency of representation by defense counsel in the cases of abortion providers, principal-participants, and accomplices. Providers had defense counsel 70% of the time, while women who had abortions had legal counsel in only 38% of the cases. Principal-participants and accomplices had legal counsel at rates similar to those of abortion providers. These circumstances might be explained by the fact that the providers usually had been previously prosecuted and convicted for abortion. Consequently, contact with the legal system had familiarized them with the necessary course of action. Moreover, provisional release from prison is harder for abortion providers to secure than for women who have had abortions, so providers need to find a lawyer in an early stage of the process. Of the 41 cases in these categories of defendants that had defense counsel, nine were defended for free, nine were assisted by lawyers from the Legal Aid Corporation, and two by court-nominated attorneys.

Bar Graph 12: Representation by Defense Cousel of Providers, Principal-participants, and Accomplices

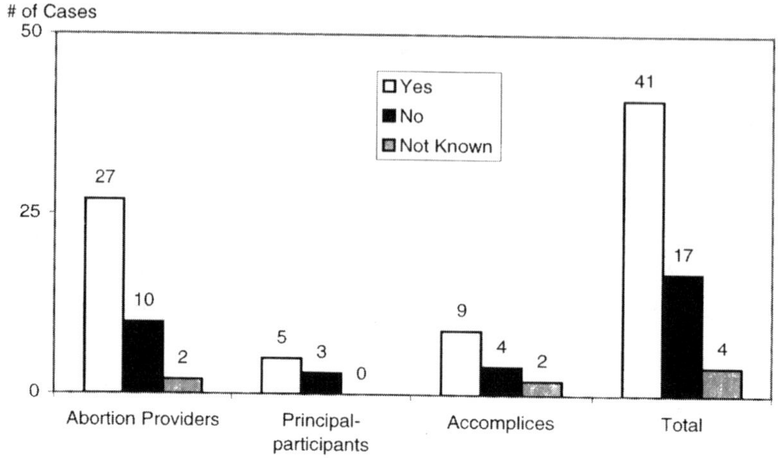

C.3 PREVENTIVE IMPRISONMENT

For many of those prosecuted for abortion, especially women who have abortions, this is their first contact with the criminal justice system. In the Chilean criminal process, it is usual for a suspect to remain in prison before the trial and the sentencing. When this incarceration is the result of a court order, it is called preventive imprisonment because its purpose is to prevent the suspect from fleeing.[108]

Many scholars agree that preventive imprisonment is used as a penalty in advance of conviction, that is, the trial and sentencing were effectively moved forward and the suspect imprisoned as a punishment.[109] When the preventive imprisonment is longer than a month, the punishment component is obviously high. It is impossible to support the notion that women accused of abortion should be imprisoned because they are a "danger" to society. Rather preventive imprisonment constitutes punishment. The advantages of alternatives to imprisonment, such as rehabilitation and avoiding exposing women to criminal behavior inside the prison, outweigh the supposed justifications of imposing an anticipated punishment.

Women who have had abortions and preventive imprisonment

Comparing cities and years (see Table 13) reveals that 57% of women who had abortions spent time in prison. Close to 48% were in prison for less than 14 days, while 10% were held for more than two months.

Of that number, most of the women remained in preventive imprisonment for two to three months. Women spent longer periods in preventive imprisonment in the years 1983 and 1984, with the exception of a woman from Temuco who spent almost seven months in jail in 1990.

None of the women accused of having abortions in the cases reviewed had a criminal record. As "first time offenders" and because abortion is "such a particular crime" as some judges say, alluding to the special circumstances that motivate women to have an abortion, many women spend little or no time in prison. To see the amount of time women who had abortions spent in preventive imprisonment in each of the cities, see Tables A-D in Annex II.

Table 13: Time Spent in Preventive Imprisonment for Women who had Abortions in All Cities

	1983	1984	1990	1991	TOTAL #	TOTAL%
# of Days						
No time in prison	8	45	3	8	64	43%
1 to 14	5	16	11	9	41	27%
15 to 30	7	5	--	--	12	8%
31 to 60	4	5	1	--	10	7%
61 to 90	--	2	3	--	5	3%
91 to 120	1	--	--	--	1	1%
121 to 150	--	1	--	--	1	1%
151 to 180	1	--	--	--	1	1%
181 to 210	--	--	--	--	--	--
More than 211	--	--	1	--	1	1%
Not Known	2	7	5	--	14	9%
Sub-total	20	36	21	9	86	57%
TOTAL	28	81	24	17	150	100%*

* The percentages are approximate and may not add up to 100%.

Providers and principal-participants in preventive imprisonment

It seems that coprincipals, that is, providers and principal-participants, were considered by courts to be, as criminal law scholars say, a menace to society. Table 15 shows that 87% of them spent time in preventive imprisonment, compared with 57% of the women who had abortions.

Abortion providers clearly spent a longer time in prison than women who had abortions. Four (9.7%) of the 29 persons whose time in preventive imprisonment is known, spent more than a year in preventive imprisonment. The overall percentage of the persons who spent more than three months in prison was 17%. The longest periods of preventive imprisonment were ordered by Santiago courts, except in one case in Temuco where an abortion provider spent more than one year in jail.

Table 14: Time spent in Preventive Imprisonment for Coprincipals and Principal-participants in all Cities

	1983	1984	1990	1991	TOTAL #	TOTAL%
# of Days						
No time in prison	3	1	2	--	6	13%
1 to 14	--	2	8	4	14	30%
15 to 30	4	2	1	--	7	15%
31 to 60	--	1	--	--	1	2%
61 to 90	--	4	1	--	5	11%
91 to 120	1	--	--	--	1	2%
121 to 150	--	1	--	--	1	2%
151 to 180	--	--	--	--	--	--
181 to 210	--	--	--	--	--	--
More than 211	4	--	2	--	6	13%
Not Known	3	3	--	--	6	13%
Sub-total	12	13	12	4	41	87%
TOTAL	15	14	14	4	47	100%*

* The percentages are approximate and may not add up to 100%.

Almost all providers who spent a year or more in prison were involved in abortion cases that had serious consequences, such as complications resulting in hysterectomies or death. Among the principal-participants, those who spent the most time in preventive imprisonment were also part of similar cases, including three cases in which the woman who had the abortion had to have a hysterectomy.

Accomplices in preventive imprisonment

Accomplices are in a similar situation to both women who had abortions and abortion providers. As Table 15 shows, 87% of accomplices were held in preventive imprisonment, a figure that is more like that of abortion providers and principal-participants than that of women who had abortions. However, the periods of time these persons remained in prison were similar to those of women who had abortions. Forty percent spent less than 14 days in jail. No accomplice spent longer than two months in jail. Under the theory that preventive imprisonment is used to punish in advance of conviction, accomplices should and did receive less time in prison than women who had abortions and coprincipals, who are the main actors in illegal abortion procedures. The accomplice who spent the longest period in prison, 54 days, was involved in a case of a woman who died as a result of the abortion. (Santiago, 1983).

Table 15: Time Spent in Preventive Imprisonment for Accomplices in all Cities

	1983	1984	1990	1991	TOTAL #	TOTAL %
# of Days						
No time in prison	--	1	1	--	2	13%
1 to 14	--	--	4	--	4	27%
15 to 30	1	1	--	--	2	13%
31 to 60	--	2	1	--	3	20%
61 to 90	--	--	--	--	--	--
91 to 120	--	--	--	--	--	--
121 to 150	--	--	--	--	--	--
151 to 180	--	--	--	--	--	--
181 to 210	--	--	--	--	--	--
More than 211	--	--	--	--	--	--
Not Known	3	1	--	--	4	27%
Sub-total	4	4	5	--	13	87%
TOTAL	4	5	6	--	15	100%*

* The percentages are approximate and may not add up to 100%.

As a result of these comparisons, it is plausible to argue that the time spent in preventive imprisonment is directly related to the concept of punishing in advance of conviction. It is proportional to the sentence that the suspects would get if they were convicted. For example, accomplices on average were in prison for an average of 20.5 days, women who had abortions 31.3 days, principal-participants 68.5 days, and providers 84.1 days.

C.4 LEGAL ARGUMENTS AND STRATEGIES USED BY THE DEFENSE

There are mainly two categories of defense used in these cases. The first one is that it was not possible for the defendant to take any other course of action, an exception provided for in Article 10 of the Criminal Code. The second line of defense is that the sentence normally imposed should be reduced. This argument is based either on mitigating circumstances, contained in Article 11 of the Criminal Code, or on the exception of *honoris causa abortion*, that is, abortion for reasons of honor or reputation, which receives a lesser punishment under Chilean criminal law.[110]

The Chilean criminal justice system does not accept any extenuating circumstances aside from those specifically provided by law. The judge plays an active part in identifying these circumstances in accordance with the Criminal Procedure Code. Article 109 establishes that: "[t]he judge must zealously investigate not only the facts and circumstances that aggravate the accused's responsibility, but also those that lessen or mitigate it."

However, Chilean law contains no other specific extenuating circumstance for abortion aside from *honoris causa*, which was mentioned above. Even so, it is always the defense's task to make sure all extenuating circumstances are investigated.

There are many reasons for a woman to terminate her pregnancy, such as the lack of support from her partner, the lack of means to support another child, fear of her parents' reaction, possible loss of employment, not wanting the child because it is the result of rape, the failure of a contraceptive method, etc. Usually it is not only one reason but the concurrence of many reasons that leads a woman to make the difficult decision to have an abortion. Defense counsel is charged with highlighting these circumstances, and finding a link between the woman's circumstances and the abstract legal rules that might be favorable to her. In the cases investigated for this report, there were three main lines of defense:

1. That the crime had not been proved because there was insufficient evidence of abortion.

2. That the fact that she was forced to have an abortion legally exempts her from responsibility.

3. That the woman had been subjected to an irresistible fear, and was thus legally exempted from responsibility.

In the event none of the strategies above was accepted, the defense argued that the punishment should be reduced, because one or more of the following extenuating circumstances was present:

1. That the same arguments used to argue that the defendant had no choice but to have an abortion be accepted as extenuating circumstances.

2. That the woman acted out of extreme grief.

3. That the woman had the abortion to protect her reputation (*honoris causa abortion*).

4. That the woman had irreproachable conduct prior to the abortion.

5. That she zealously tried to repair the damage.

C.5 RESULTS OF CRIMINAL PROSECUTIONS FOR ABORTION

Results of the prosecutions of women who had abortions

Not every criminal prosecution ends with a conviction or acquittal. In fact most criminal prosecutions for abortion in Chile end with a "suspension decree" (*resolución de sobreseimiento*), which could be temporary or definitive, and results in the investigation being either terminated or suspended. The suspension decree is an "abnormal" way of ending the criminal justice process, since there is no court decision that acquits or convicts the accused parties, except in the case of a definitive suspension decree.[111] However, some legal scholars consider a suspension decree to be a form of acquittal, since there is no criminal record. The court can decide to suspend the proceedings at any stage during the criminal process, even when there has been a conviction and a sentence, but the defendant cannot be found to notify him or her. There are other forms of ending the criminal process. For example, the court may decide that it lacks jurisdiction, that is, that it is incompetent to hear the case, and that the case must be remitted to the appropriate court.

In this report we found that the trend in all cities was to end abortion prosecutions with a suspension decree. In almost every city, prosecutions for abortion ended in the following manner: 28% in a conviction, 2% due to lack of jurisdiction (competency) of the court, and 70% in suspension. The main reason for issuing the suspension decree was that the Institute of Forensic Medicine[112] could not confirm or deny the abortion procedure. In such cases, according to Article 409(1) of the Criminal Procedure Code, the criminal process must be suspended. The report of forensic doctors is determinative of whether the suspension decree must be issued. These reports usually state that, except in cases where the pregnancy was very advanced, the women examined showed no signs of pregnancy or abortion, and that the only reason to believe there had been an abortion was the defendant's declaration as stated in her medical record.

Chart 16: Results of Prosecutions of Women Who Had Abortions in All Cities (Total # of Cases: 150)

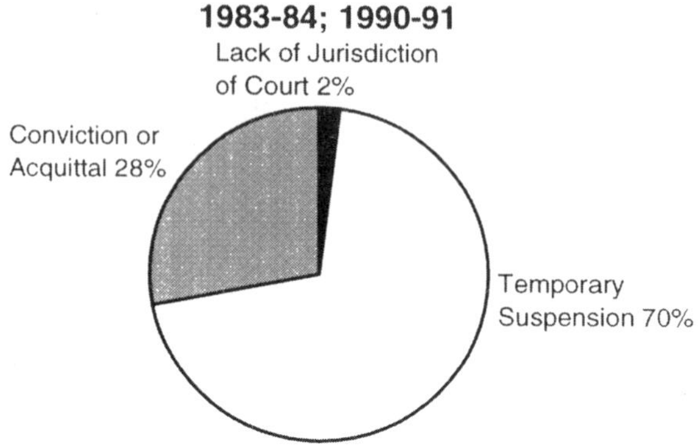

All the suspensions were temporary, resulting in the suspension of the criminal process and not in its termination. In almost all the cases, the case was suspended to wait for better evidence, in accordance with the Criminal Code.[113] In some cases, the temporary suspensions resulted in absurd situations. A Santiago woman was reported in 1984, two years after her stay in the maternity ward with signs of abortion. Because she did not show up for the trial, she was declared in contempt of court in accordance with the Criminal Procedure Code[114] and the case was suspended. In 1989, seven years after the abortion and five years after being reported to the Intelligence Police, the Institute of Forensic Medicine stated, naturally, that it had found no signs of an abortion. The court decided, after taking all the customary statements, to decree once more the temporary suspension of the case. It is hard to understand why, if after seven years there was no longer any way of continuing the investigation, the judge would consider it necessary to suspend the investigation and continue it some time in the future.

A woman from Arica went through a similar situation in 1987, when she was arrested as she was leaving the country, years after her presumed abortion. Her lawyer successfully interposed the *recurso de amparo*, a kind of writ similar to the writ of habeas corpus that is used to protect constitutional rights. The lawyer argued that the order for her arrest was invalid since she was a minor when the supposed abortion took place, in 1983. During the supposed time of the pregnancy, the woman had been sent to a state home for children, since because of her parent's advanced age, they could not care for her.

Table 17: Incoming Cases, Convictions, Acquittals and Temporary Suspensions in Abortion Cases from 1982 to 1991

	Incoming Cases	Convictions	Acquittals	Temporary Suspension
1991	218	24	8	134
1989	294	45	10	181
1988	282	51	17	171
1987	354	62	16	220
1986	312	46	22	217
1985	396	69	8	219
1984	503	66	23	240
1983	605	66	18	230
1982	643	81	23	207

Source: National Statistics Institute, Justice Yearbook, years 1989, 1988, 1987, 1986, 1985, 1984, 1983, 1982, Ministry for Economy, Promotion and Reconstruction, published in various years, and unpublished statistics for 1991 of the National Statistics Institute. 1990 not available.

In this study, in Santiago 22% of the cases ended in conviction or acquittal, compared to 33% in Valparíso and 25% in Arica. The only city where a case did not end in acquittal, conviction, or temporary suspension, was in Santiago, where 3% of the cases ended in a declaration of lack of jurisdiction of the court.

Results of the prosecutions of providers and accomplices

Chart 18 illustrates the situation of the persons prosecuted as providers and as principal-participants in abortion. Thirty-six percent of the cases resulted in conviction or acquittal while 62% were temporarily suspended. Chart 19 shows that prosecutions against accomplices had almost identical results: 33% of the cases resulted in conviction or acquittal, and 66% were temporarily suspended.

Chart 18: Results of Prosecutions of Abortion Providers and Principal-Providers in All Cities (Total # of Cases: 47)

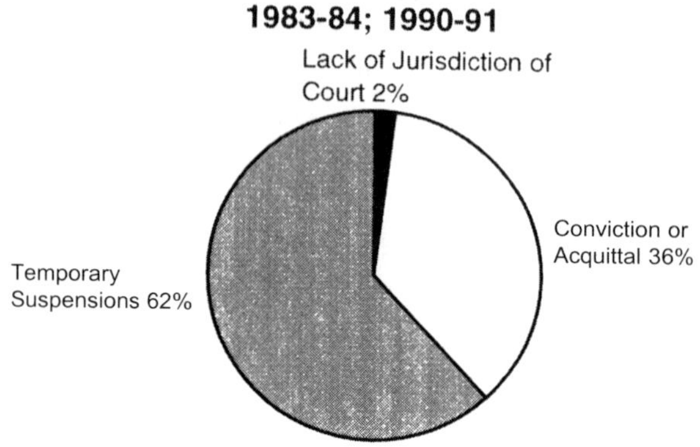

Chart 19: Results of Prosecutions of Accomplices in All Cities (Total # of Cases: 15)

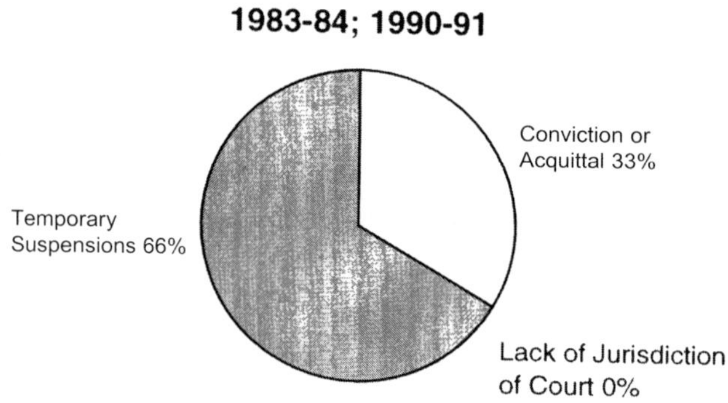

Convictions and acquittals

Chart 20 shows that of those women who terminated their pregnancies whose cases were not temporarily suspended but went to trial, the majority were convicted. Twenty-four percent of them were acquitted by the trial court, while 10% were convicted at trial, but were acquitted by the court of appeals. Consequently, one-third of the women in this study who were tried for abortion were acquitted. Sixteen percent of all women prosecuted for abortion were convicted, while the great majority had their cases suspended (70%), and 9% were acquitted. In the same chart, the category "Not Known" corresponds to three cases whose results are unknown.

Chart 20: Convictions and Acquittals of Women Who Had Abortions in All Cities (Total # of Cases: 42)

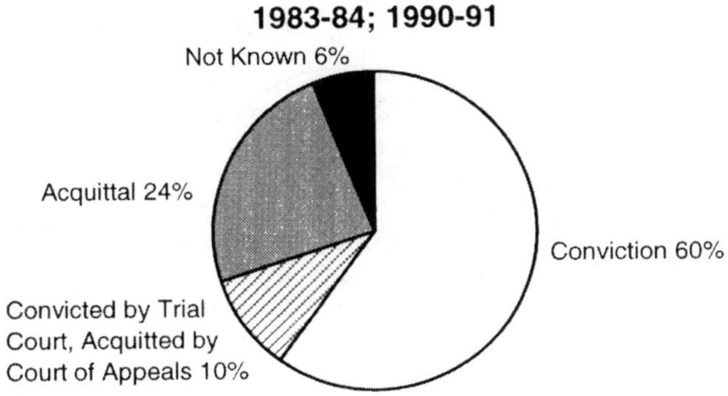

Chart 21 shows that abortion providers and principal-participants who were actually tried had an experience similar to that of the women accused of having abortions. Sixty-nine percent were convicted, 24% acquitted, and 7% convicted at trial and acquitted by the Court of Appeals, for a total of 31% of acquittals. If all cases of providers and principal-participants are taken as a whole, 42% were convicted, 36% had their cases temporarily suspended, and 19% were acquitted.

Chart 21: Convictions and Acquittals of Providers and Principal-Participants in All Cities (Total # of Cases: 29)

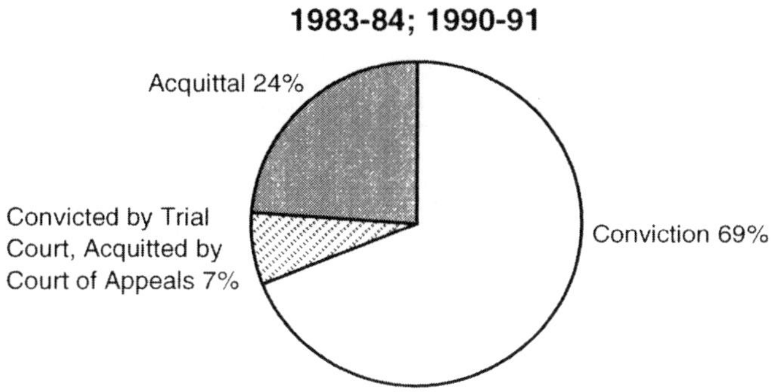

Chart 22 shows what happened to the accomplices. Sixty percent of the cases that were not temporarily suspended ended in conviction and 40%

in acquittal. In 40% of all cases, accomplices were convicted, 27% were acquitted and 33% had their cases temporarily suspended.

Chart 22: Convictions and Acquittals of Accomplices in all Cities (Total # of Cases: 10)

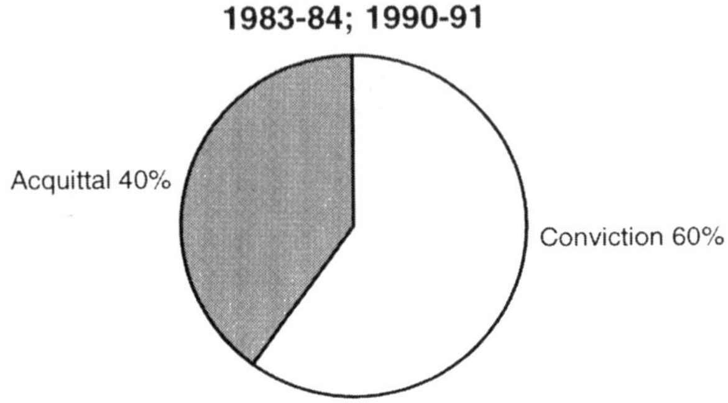

Penalties upon conviction

Under the Chilean Criminal Code, the penalty for abortion varies according to the role the individual played in the crime. The woman who has consented to her own abortion is punished with a category of punishment called "lesser imprisonment of the highest degree." The applicable prison term would range from three years and a day to five years. If she had the abortion to protect her honor, the so-called *honoris causa abortion*, the applicable punishment is from 541 days to three years. Third parties who are not physicians who provide abortions are subject to less severe penalties than physicians: the penalty is from 541 days to three years. If the abortion provider is a physician, then he or she receives a longer sentence.

Chart 23 illustrates the length of sentences imposed on women who had abortions. Most of them were sentenced to 541 days of prison. All the women who had abortions were eligible for alternative punishments such as conditional deferral of the sentence or parole, meaning they did not have to spend any additional time in prison. See, however, the previous section on "Preventive Imprisonment": 57% of all women prosecuted for having abortions spent time in preventive imprisonment.

Chart 23: Length of Sentence of Women Who Had Abortions in All Cities (Total # of Cases: 20)

1983-84; 1990-91

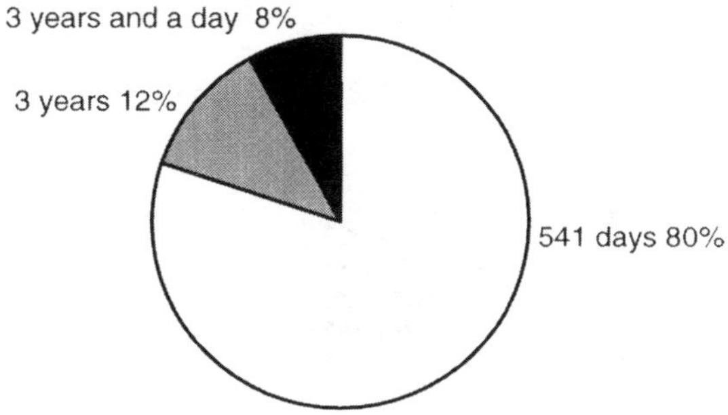

The alternative punishments prescribed by Law 18,216 are conditional deferral of the sentence, parole, and nightly detention. The first alternative punishment referred to above is for prison sentences that are not longer than three years, the second for those from two to five years, and the third for those shorter than three years. There are other conditions that must also be met for one of these to apply: lack of a criminal record, a favorable opinion on the part of the Chilean Police in regard to the defendant's rehabilitation, and that the defendant have a known activity or profession. If the defendant violates any of these conditions, she must complete her sentence in jail.

Most abortion providers in this study were sentenced to 541 days in prison. However the percentage—65%—is lower than that of women who had abortions. The range of sentence length is greater for abortion providers than for women who had abortions. Unlike the women who had abortions, not all the providers could benefit from Law 18,216, since many of them had previous convictions.

As discussed above, abortion providers spent more time in preventive imprisonment, which seemed to function as an additional punishment. Even those judges who are personally opposed to abortion tend to be more understanding of the woman's position. As several judges recognized, having an abortion can be explained in many ways, and often the explanations are very moving. The provider, however, is perceived as someone who is out to make a profit, even though in many cases, as can been seen from the cases in this study, these individuals, especially women who provided abortions, did so free of charge to help other women in need.

Chart 24: Length of Sentence of Abortion Providers and Principal-participants in All Cities (Total # of Cases: 20)

1983-84; 1990-91

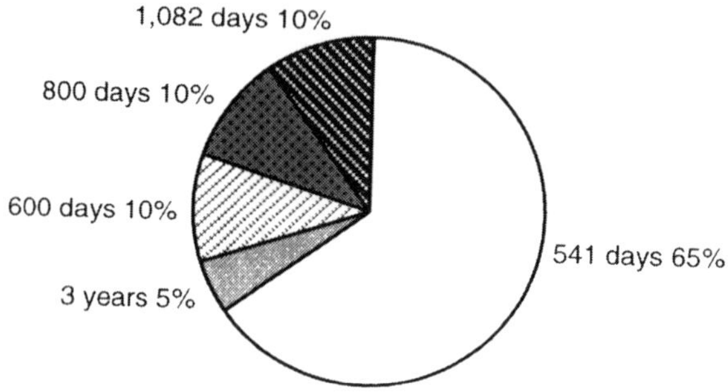

The law regards accomplices as having secondary responsibility, and their sentences reflect this situation. Chart 25 shows that four out of the six accomplices were sentenced to 61 days in prison, and their sentences were conditionally deferred for a year, under the oversight of a Penitentiary Board. The absence of clear and uniform criteria in the application of sentences is seen in the following examples: the accomplice sentenced to more than 200 days was involved in an abortion that resulted in death. In another case, the judge sentenced an accomplice to 541 days in prison even though the abortion did not result in serious medical complications.

Chart 25: Length of Sentence of Accomplices in All Cities (Total # of Cases: 6)

1983-84; 1990-91

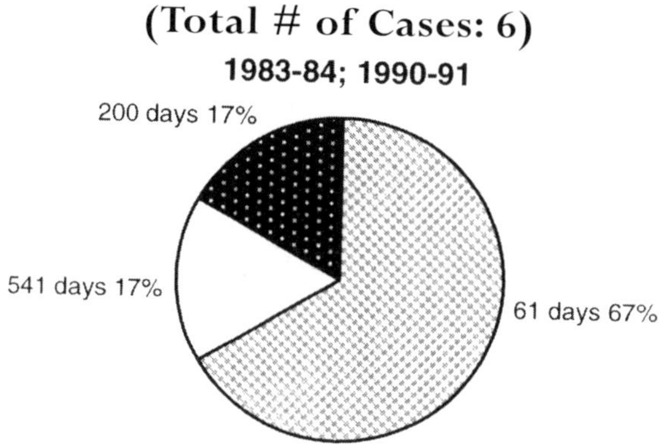

Marcela, 66 years old, is an abortion provider who has been in jail three different times.

"I took a three-year nursing course — not first aid, nursing — and there I had to do training rotations at the police stations and at Emergency Room Four.... At the police station I had, I was assigned specifically to gynecology, and that was one of the first things I learned, seeing the women in really bad shape, with many problems, a lot of problems. We talked, I would go over and chat, since I was doing my training I wasn't really working. I came up and chatted with them about the problems they had, why they had had an abortion, then, well, I never thought it would be a job, just to help a little, you know ... Because they come to me so overwhelmed, the woman that is married but it's impossible to have another child because she is working, or because her husband is ill. Or the girl who is single, and she can't because she is studying, because her life would be ruined, although it shouldn't be that way because a child is a blessing from God. But seeing it from the point of view of the problems there are and that there were in those years, and now, now its worse, we have gone back a

whole bunch of years.... The first time I did it was for a cousin, who, I'm not ashamed to say, was a prostitute, and she was very unhappy because she had three children already, and it's a hard life, that world of prostitution.... So she was the first one, I helped her, let's say, and then I went on, you know, then it was a neighbor's. And one day they say, no, you have to charge something, at least a little.... I didn't take it like that either, I always think that we [meaning the poor] cannot say anybody is not in need you know, so I charged only what I needed. Sometimes I didn't get anything, usually, sometimes I got some earrings or some little ring as a pledge, and they never came back, so it was like a present, and in those hard times we had [meaning the dictatorship], I started charging, but not too much either."

Excerpted from an interview with Marcela conducted by Patricia Olea, January 1998.

CHAPTER IV: SOCIAL AND ECONOMIC CHARACTERISTICS OF WOMEN PROSECUTED FOR ABORTION AND OF ABORTION PROVIDERS

This chapter summarizes the social and economic data on the women prosecuted for abortion as well as on the abortion providers. In Chapter III, only the individuals actually prosecuted for abortion were discussed, whereas in this chapter all women who had abortions are included, even those women who were not prosecuted because they were minors or "victims" of abortions.

A. AGE OF THE WOMEN WHO HAD ABORTIONS

Sixty-one percent of the women in this study were between 18 and 29 years old. Women aged 30 to 41 comprised 26% of the sample, while those older than 42 were only 2% (see Table 26). Studies conducted in the 1960s and the first half of the 1970s indicated that women who had abortions were usually young, between 25 and 29, married or cohabiting, with one to three children, and that they had had previous abortions associated with contraceptive failure.[115]

Minors (those younger than 18) represented 8% of all women in this study who had abortions. None of them were prosecuted, because they lack the legal capacity to be criminal defendants. However, in spite of being minors, they were placed at the disposal of the court, except in those cases where they were victims of an abortion without their consent.

These facts seem to indicate that the statistical curve of women who have abortions is changing — more younger women are resorting to abortion. Considering that, as Chapter II describes, there is inadequate access to contraceptive methods in Chile, the government should be regarded as responsible for unwanted pregnancies among young women.

Table 26: Percentage Distribution of Cases by Age and City

	Santiago	Valparaíso	Arica	Temuco	Total
Age					
less than 14	1%	6%	---	---	2%
15-17	3%	3%	28%	6%	6%
18-20	15%	20%	6%	18%	15%
21-23	18%	13%	6%	35%	18%
24-26	13%	23%	11%	6%	14%
27-29	16%	10%	17%	6%	14%
30-32	10%	---	11%	---	7%
33-35	5%	10%	6%	6%	6%
36-38	11%	6%	6%	6%	9%
39-41	4%	6%	---	6%	4%
42-44	1%	---	---	---	1%
45-47	1%	---	6%	---	2%
Not Known	1%	3%	6%	12%	3%
Total	100%	100%	100%	100%	100%*

*Percentages are approximate and may not add up to 100%.

B. MARITAL STATUS

Chilean law recognizes three kinds of "marital status": married, single, and widowed. Unlike most Latin American countries, it does not recognize *uniones de hecho* (domestic partnerships), separation (where a couple is legally married but does not live as a couple anymore), or divorce. Chile may possibly enter the next millennium as the only country in the world without a divorce law.[116] Those who are legally married and later have their marriage legally annulled are considered legally single. Annulments are sometimes granted through a formal loophole, such as the supposed incompetence of an official at the Civil Registrar's Office. That is, a sympathetic judge can annul a marriage because the couple and a handful of witnesses say the couple never lived at the address written on the marriage license.[117] This report thus includes categories not recognized by Chilean law: single and cohabiting, widowed and cohabiting, and separated and cohabiting.

A majority of the people prosecuted for abortion were single, followed closely by married people. These statistics, as explained above, do not properly account for women who are cohabiting. As Table 27 shows, women in a stable relationship (married, single and cohabiting, separated and cohabiting, and widowed and cohabiting) collectively represented 43% of all women who had abortions. Forty-nine percent of the women in the sample were either single, widowed, or separated; 44% of the sample were single women.

Table 27: Marital Status of Women Who Had Abortions by Year in all Cities

	1983		1984		1990		1991		Total	Total
Status	#	%	#	%	#	%	#	%	#	%
Single	16	53	35	41	13	48	6	35	70	44
Cohabiting and Single	7	23	9	11	3	11	1	6	20	13
Married	5	17	23	27	4	15	8	47	40	25
Cohabiting and Separated	---	---	3	4	1	4	1	6	5	3
Separated	1	3	3	4	3	11	---	---	7	4
Cohabiting and Widowed	1	3	1	1	---	---	1	6	3	2
Widowed	---	---	1	1	---	---	---	---	1	1
Not Known	---	---	10	12	3	11	---	---	13	8
Total	30	100	85	100	27	100	17	100	159	100

C. EDUCATIONAL LEVEL

In Chile, primary education is mandatory, and it includes eight years of school, from age 6 to 13 or 14. Public school is supposed to be free, but contrary to this principle, schools require payments for a series of expenses, such as matriculation fees, Parent's Center contributions, and the cost of mandatory school uniforms.

This report includes a category that shows whether or not a person is illiterate. This category, denominated "reads and writes," is used by courts to establish whether the defendant should receive copies of her file or whether it should be read to her. This report also distinguishes between complete and incomplete primary and secondary school education. This report does not include a category for technical or professional education, since no one included in this study had such an education, or if they had it, it was not in the court records.

Of women who had abortions in the four cities, without taking account of age, Table 28 shows two very high rates of 21%, corresponding to women who did not complete their primary education, and to those who could only "read and write." Second place is held by those women who had a few years of secondary education but did not finish (19% of the total). Only 9% of the women had finished 12 years of education. Seven percent were illiterate.

Table 28: Education Level in all the Cases Reviewed

	1983		1984		1990		1991		Total	
Level of Education	#	%	#	%	#	%	#	%	#	%
Illiterate	2	7%	7	8%	2	7%	1	6%	12	7%
Incomplete Primary	1	3%	23	27%	5	19%	4	24%	33	21%
Complete Primary	3	10%	3	3%	1	4%	2	12%	9	6%
Incomplete Secondary	7	23%	13	15%	6	22%	4	24%	30	19%
Complete Secondary	4	13%	4	5%	4	15%	2	12%	14	9%
Reads and Writes	10	33%	16	19%	4	15%	3	18%	33	21%
Not Known	3	10%	19	23%	5	19%	1	6%	28	18%
Total	30	100%	85	100%	27	100%	17	100%	159	100%

The total percentage of women whose educational level was between some years of primary education to incomplete secondary was 55%. This figure does not include the "reads and writes" category, which added to the previous figure gives a total of 76%. Temuco had the lowest percentage of educated women: 18% of the women were illiterate, and 66% had between one year of primary education and complete secondary school education. Although no woman with college or technical education was found among the court records, some might be found in the "reads and writes" category, since some of them had occupations that could require some kind of post-high school education. For example, there was a woman who was listed in court records as having "completed midlevel studies," another who was a secretary, and a third who said her education was "technical-social," leaving unclear her precise level of education.

It is possible to conclude from the above data that women prosecuted for abortion in Chile as a group have little formal education. The majority has either elementary education or incomplete secondary school education, indicating a poor sector of the population.

D. NUMBER OF CHILDREN

The number of children women already have is an important variable insofar as abortion is closely related to unwanted pregnancy. When women already have the number of children they want, unplanned pregnancies might result in abortion, especially when the woman's economic conditions are unfavorable. A 1991 study indicated that from a group of 2,300 pregnant women, 28.5% of the women did not want the pregnancy and 38.4% had mixed feelings about being pregnant.[118] It is estimated that, in Chile, 44% of all pregnancies are unwanted.[119]

In the cases reviewed, the results from different cities show that the highest percentages of abortion were found among women who already had one or two children. Of women who had children, the total percentage of both categories was 61%. Including the percentage of women who have three children, the total of all three categories is 76%. It is interesting to note that in one of the studies mentioned above, the relationship between pregnancy and previous births shows that the desire to have children drops significantly from the fourth pregnancy on.[120]

Chart 29: Number of Children per Woman in All Cities

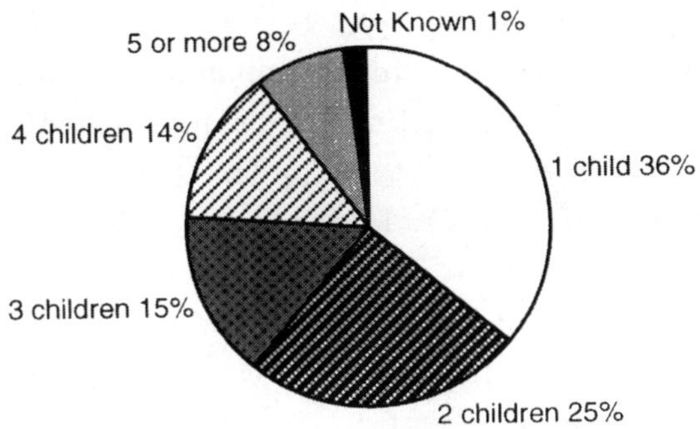

There is also a relationship between education and number of children: women with less education have on average more children than more educated women. The relationship between education and number of children in the cases reviewed is an example of this. Table 30 shows the distribution of children among women according to their education. Although the education of 36% of the women could not be determined exactly (the categories "reads and writes" and "not known" each represent 18% of the total), it is possible to conclude that 43% of the women with children were illiterate or had only incomplete or complete primary education. In addition, the 22 illiterate women comprised 55% of the women with four or more children.

Table 30: Number of Children and Level of Education in All Cities

	1 Child		2 Children		3 Children		4 Children		5 or more		Total	
Education	#	%	#	%	#	%	#	%	#	%	#	%
Illiterate	1	1%	---	---	---	---	3	3%	4	4%	8	8%
Incomplete Primary	11	11%	5	5%	6	6%	3	3%	2	2%	27	28%
Complete Primary	2	2%	4	4%	1	1%	---	---	---	---	7	7%
Incomplete Secondary	7	7%	2	2%	3	3%	2	2%	---	---	14	15%
Complete Secondary	4	4%	2	2%	---	---	---	---	---	---	6	6%
Reads and Writes	7	7%	4	4%	3	3%	3	3%	---	---	17	18%
Not Known	3	3%	7	7%	2	2%	3	3%	2	2%	17	18%
TOTAL	35	36%	24	25%	15	16%	14	15%	8	8%	96	100%

* The percentages are approximate and may not add up to 100%.

Women who completed secondary education tended to have one or two children, representing 6% of all women with children. Almost a third of the women with one child had not finished primary school education. Likewise, women with an incomplete secondary school education accounted for 20% of those who had one child. Within the same group of women with some high school education, 3% had three children, 2% had two children, and 2% had four. Also within this group of women with incomplete high school education, there was a higher percentage of women who had no children (13 out of 45, almost 29%). Next in frequency of women without children were those women with a complete high school education, totalling 16%.

E. ECONOMIC ACTIVITY

The group of women who had abortions was composed mostly of working women (47%) and women who had no paid job (41%). This second group was composed of housewives (29%) and students (12%).

Table 31: Economic Activity of the Women in All Cities by Year

	1983		1984		1990		1991		TOTAL	
	#	%	#	%	#	%	#	%	#	%
No Remunerated Labor										
Housewife	7	23%	24	28%	8	30%	7	41%	46	29%
Student	5	17%	7	8%	4	15%	3	18%	19	12%
SUB-TOTAL	12	40%	31	36%	12	45%	10	59%	65	41%
Remunerated Labor										
Domestic Servant	5	17%	9	11%	3	11%	---	---	17	11%
Worker	2	7%	10	12%	2	7%	1	6%	15	9%
Seamstress	1	3%	5	6%	1	4%	1	6%	8	5%
Temp. Agricultural Worker	1	3%	3	4%	1	4%	2	12%	7	4%
Employee	3	10%	1	1%	1	4%	---	---	5	4%
Hairdresser	---	---	4	5%	1	4%	---	---	5	3%
Sales/Merchant	1	3%	3	4%	---	---	---	---	4	3%
Nanny	1	3%	2	2%	---	---	---	---	3	2%
Midwife	1	3%	---	---	1	4%	1	6%	3	2%
Waitress	---	---	1	1%	---	---	---	---	1	1%
Dancer	---	---	1	1%	---	---	---	---	1	1%
Prostitute	---	---	1	1%	---	---	---	---	1	1%
Occupation Unknown	---	---	2	2%	---	---	2	12%	4	3%
SUB-TOTAL	15	50%	42	49%	10	37%	7	41%	74	47%
Not Known	3	10%	12	14%	5	19%	---	---	20	13%
TOTAL	30	100%	85	100%	27	100%	17	100%	159	100%

*The percentages are approximate and may not add up to 100%.

F. SOCIAL AND ECONOMIC STATUS OF ABORTION PROVIDERS

One of the characteristics of abortion services for poor women was that the providers tended to live close to the women's home. Women often resolved their needs in universal and shared traditions transmitted from generation to generation. It is perhaps a logical consequence that most abortion providers were women: out of the 31 persons prosecuted as abortion providers, 79% were women.

While female abortion providers tended to be housewives, the males who provided abortions tended to have other paid jobs. Those female abortion providers who did work tended to do so in jobs similar to those of traditional midwives, such as nurses, health care practitioners, and other jobs involving caring for the sick. Women providers in these kinds of jobs comprised 45% of all women who were employed, and 26% of all women providers and principal-participants. Forty percent of male providers on the other hand were practitioners, nurses, or paramedics.

The rest worked as drivers, construction workers, merchants, and employees. Two of the employees were the women's partners, and were tried as principal-participants: one was a policeman (Santiago, 1983), the other an accountant (Arica, 1984), and the third one a photographer (Valparaiso, 1991).

In general, abortion providers were women as poor as those who asked them for help. Male providers, unlike the women, used more aggressive methods, including medical instruments, and they ended to have some level of education in health services.

From an interview by the Open Forum on September 25, 1997, in the "Chin Chin" prison facility in Puerto Montt, Chile. On that date, there were 22 women imprisoned there for abortion-related offenses, who were accused of having abortions or providing abortions to other women.

Carmen is 20-years-old and a domestic worker. After she got pregnant by a married man, she was forced by him to have an abortion in very poor conditions. The man was worried that if she decided to have the baby he could be blackmailed in the future and this would cause him problems with his wife and children.

CHAPTER V: RECOMMENDATIONS

A. AT THE NATIONAL LEVEL

1. The Chilean government should ensure that women do not risk their lives or their physical and mental health because of the prohibition on abortion in Chile. Chile should implement the following legal and policy changes in order to end the persecution of women prosecuted for abortion and to ensure the reproductive health of Chilean women:

- The separation between church and state should be respected. The state should assume its secular responsibility to take action on public health and social justice issues. It is recommended that it begin by allowing therapeutic abortion.

- The law that penalizes women for having abortions should be repealed.

- As long as abortion continues to be criminalized in Chile, we recommend that public health services should provide both counseling and medical treatment for women who have had abortions and those with incomplete abortions.

- The state should provide all the population of reproductive age with the full range of reproductive health services and information and education related to reproductive health, in order to prevent unwanted pregnancies.

- There is no specific population policy in Chile. Neither is there a clear government position on the relationship between population and development. Moreover, there is a lack of up to date information on fertility rates and the reproductive health of the population. The government should institute a national fertility and reproductive behavior survey. In addition, it should initiate a process that, with the active participation of the women's health movement, would eventually create an explicit population policy.

- Chile should fulfill its obligation to provide reports regarding its implementation of the international treaties it has ratified. This would show the contradiction between the reality of Chile's criminal laws and the development of international human rights law, particularly in relation to the progress at various recent world conferences that dealt with women's reproductive rights.

- The government should create a three-tiered commission, comprising representatives from the government, the United Nations, and civil society, in order to monitor Chile's progress in implementing the Cairo Conference commitments.

- The government's National Report on Population and Development drafted for the Cairo Conference does not fully cover the issue of abortion. It assumes the Chilean population never resorts to abortion as a method of family planning, and it does not give a conceptual framework to address the real dimensions of the problem posed by abortion or any way to resolve it. Therefore, research should be undertaken on the issue of abortion as a method of contraception, and on the difficulty women have accessing other contraceptive methods.

2. The state should ensure the right to privacy in the provision of health services. In order to do so it should carry out the following actions:

- Revise the Health Code provision that obligates or permits physicians to report women who seek their help after having had an abortion.

- Implement government policies ensuring that laws on patient confidentiality will be observed in public hospitals.

3. The state should ensure the right to defense counsel to all those who cannot afford an attorney. Moreover, those criminal procedures, such as preventive imprisonment, which violate the right to due process and the right to be presumed innocent also must be reviewed and revised.

B. AT THE INTERNATIONAL LEVEL:
Recommendations for international donors

- International and regional development agencies, as well as international donor agencies financing public health programs in Chile, should be party to the implementation of comprehensive family planning and pregnancy prevention programs in order to decrease the need for abortion.

- The aforementioned organizations should monitor health services in general, and reproductive health services in particular, ensuring that they are offered without any form of discrimination. In order to protect women's health and lives, no one should be discriminated against regardless of the reason for seeking health care, including those women suffering from complications caused by clandestine abortions.

Role of the universal and regional human rights systems

• The Human Rights Committee, the Committee on the Elimination of All Forms of Discrimination Against Women, as well as other bodies that monitor international human rights treaties ratified by Chile, should scrutinize Chilean legislation, particularly on abortion, to encourage the repeal of those laws that violate women's human rights.

• The organs of the Inter-American human rights system should likewise contribute to the repeal of restrictive and discriminatory abortion laws in Chile, as well as to the elimination of the prosecution and imprisonment of Chilean women for abortion. The role of these organs is to demand the protection of the rights guaranteed by regional treaties, particularly the American Convention on Human Rights and the Convention of Belém do Pará.

• In order to fulfill the Chilean government's commitments agreed to at the Cairo and Beijing Conferences, the bodies comprising the human rights systems, both international and regional, should demand the fulfillment of the civil, political, economic, and social rights of women. The human rights system should particularly demand the fulfillment of the rights that guarantee women's access to better sexual and reproductive health, and to the possibility of making informed choices regarding their reproductive lives free from discrimination, coercion, and violence.

ANNEX 1: METHODOLOGY USED IN THIS INVESTIGATION

A. GATHERING DATA

This stage of research consisted of reviewing the incoming case records for the Arica, Valaparaíso, Temuco, and Santiago courts, in order to identify the abortion cases and their file numbers in the years covered. Then we requested access to court records. We gathered the relevant information from these records and entered it into a database, including the defendant's statement, the evidence gathered by the police, statements by doctors and midwives, medical records, medical files when they were part of the court records, the briefs presented by the defense, and the significant decisions of the court itself.

B. RECORDING DATA

We collected the following information from the typical court file:

- Age, marital status, occupation, education, number of children, and procedure used for terminating the pregnancy.
- Circumstances surrounding the abortion.
- Time spent in preventive imprisonment.
- Access to and type of legal defense.
- Result of the criminal process.
- Date and manner in which the abortion was discovered and reported.
- Health consequences of the abortion, if any.
- Court and file number of the case.

This data was tabulated individually for each person. The information related to age, marital status, occupation, education, and number of children was analyzed separately for women who obtained abortions, abortion providers and third parties involved in the procedure, separating women who had abortions from abortion providers. The rest of the information was analyzed thematically.

C. DIFFICULTIES ENCOUNTERED IN THE RESEARCH

The main difficulties encountered during this investigation were:

- Excessive bureaucratic procedures to obtain the information, which slowed down the execution of the project.

- Difficulty in physically locating the relevant files, because of the inefficient filing system of court records in each city.

- Lack of infrastructure and of space in the Santiago courts, making access to public information difficult.

- Damaged incoming record books of cases and other documents because of their excessive use by the public. One appalling example of this was that three months of a particular year were missing from the books. The record books for incoming cases are particularly important, because that is where the record of each case is kept.

ANNEX 2

Table A: Time women who had abortions spent in preventive imprisonment in Santiago

	1983	1984	1990	1991	TOTAL	
# of Days						
No Time	2	38	1	2	43	48%
1 to 14	1	12	4	3	20	22%
15 to 30	6	4	--	--	10	11%
31 to 60	3	3	1	--	7	8%
61 to 90	--	1	2	--	3	3%
91 to 120	1	--	--	--	1	1%
121 to 150	--	--	--	--	--	--
151 to 180	--	--	--	--	--	--
181 to 210	--	--	--	--	--	--
More than 211	--	--	--	--	--	--
Not Known	1	5	--	--	6	7%
Sub-total	12	25	7	3	47	52%
TOTAL	14	63	8	5	90	100%*

*The percentages are approximate and may not add up to 100%.

Table B: Time women who had abortions spent in preventive imprisonment in Valparaiso

	1983	1984	1990	1991	TOTAL	
# of Days						
No Time	2	1	2	3	8	30%
1 to 14	2	3	3	6	14	52%
15 to 30	1	1	--	--	2	7%
31 to 60	--	--	--	--	--	--
61 to 90	--	--	--	-	--	--
91 to 120	--	--	--	-	--	--
121 to 150	--	--	--	--	--	--
151 to 180	--	--	--	--	--	--
181 to 210	--	--	--	--	--	--
More than 211	--	--	--	--	--	--
Not Known	--	2	1	--	3	11%
Sub-total	3	6	4	6	19	70%
TOTAL	5	7	6	9	27	100%*

* The percentages are approximate and may not add up to 100%.

Table C: Time women who had abortions spent in preventive imprisonment in Arica

	1983	1984	1990	1991	TOTAL	
# of Days						
No Time	2	6	--	1	9	56%
1 to 14	1	--	3	--	4	25%
15 to 30	--	--	--	--	--	--
31 to 60	--	2	--	--	2	13%
61 to 90	--	1	--	--	1	6%
91 to 120	--	--	--	--	--	--
121 to 150	--	--	--	--	--	--
151 to 180	--	--	--	--	--	--
181 to 210	--	--	--	--	--	--
More than 211	--	--	--	--	--	--
Not Known	--	--	--	--	--	--
Sub-total	1	3	3	--	7	44%
TOTAL	3	9	3	1	16	100%*

* The percentages are approximate and may not add up to 100%.

Table D: Time women who had abortions spent in preventive imprisonment in Temuco

	1983	1984	1990	1991	TOTAL	
# of Days						
No Time	2	--	--	2	4	24%
1 to 14	1	1	1	--	3	18%
15 to 30	--	--	--	--	--	--
31 to 60	1	--	--	--	1	6%
61 to 90	--	--	1	--	1	6%
91 to 120	--	--	--	--	--	--
121 to 150	--	1	--	--	1	6%
151 to 180	1	--	--	--	1	6%
181 to 210	--	--	--	--	--	--
More than 211	--	--	1	--	1	6%
Not Known	1	--	4	--	5	29%
Sub-total	4	2	7	--	13	76%
TOTAL	6	2	7	2	17	100%

* The percentages are approximate and may not add up to 100%.

ENDNOTES

1 The Alan Guttmacher Institute, *Aborto clandestino: Una realidad latinoamericana [Clandestine Abortion: A Latin American Reality]*, p. 5, 1994.

2 Ibid., p. 24.

3 U.N., Department of Economic and Social Development, Abortion Policies: A Global Review, Vol. I, 1992 (40% of maternal mortality in Chile is a consequence of abortion).

4 Ibid., p. 7.

5 Ibid.

6 Ibid., p. 8-9.

7 Ibid., p. 9.

8 Lidia Casas Becerra, *Mujeres procesadas por Aborto [Women Prosecuted for Abortion]*, Open Forum for Reproductive Health and Rights, in collaboration with the Center for Reproductive Law and Policy, Santiago, 1996.

9 Universal Declaration, Article 2.

10 Covenant on Civil and Political Rights, Article 2.1.

11 Covenant on Economic and Social Rights, Article 2.2.

12 The Convention on the Elimination of All Forms of Discrimination Against Women [Women's Convention] (website visited March 20 1998) < http://www.un.org/dpcsd/daw/conven.htm >.

13 Teheran Proclamation Article 15, Final Act of the International Human Rights Conference, Teheran, Iran, Mayo 12, 1968, Res. IX, U.N. Doc A/CONF. 33/41 (1968), in U.N. Department of Public Information, *The United Nations and the Advancement of Women 1945-1995*, pp. 167-169, U.N. Doc. DPI/1679 (1995).

14 Teheran Proclamation, Article 16.

15 The Vienna Declaration and Program for Action provides: "The human rights of women and girls are an inalienable, integral, and indivisible part of universal human rights. The full and equal participation of women in political, civil, economic, and cultural life, at the national, regional, and international levels, and the erradication of all forms of discrimination on the grounds of sex are priority objectives of the international community." Vienna Declaration and Program for Action, section I, paragraph 18.

16 Cairo Programme of Action, paragraph 7.2.

17 Ibid.

18 Ibid., paragraph 8.25

19 Ibid.

20 Beijing Platform, paragraph 106(k).

21 Cecilia Medina Quiroga, "El Derecho Internacional De Los Derechos Humanos y el Ordenamiento Jurídico Chileno" ["International Law on Human Rights and the Chilean Legal System"] in *Constitución, Tratados y Derechos Esenciales [Constitution, Treaties and Essential Rights]* p. 36 (1994). Article 32, No. 17 of the Constitution gives the President the special power to "negotiate; conclude, sign and ratify the treaties he deems to be in the country's interest ...." Article 50.1 of the Constitution adds that before ratifying a treaty, the president must submit the treaty to Congress for approval. The provision provides: "The following are exclusive functions of Congress: (1) To approve or reject the international treaties that the President of the Republic presents for approval prior to ratification. The approval of a treaty must follow the same procedure as the approval of a law."

22 Ibid., pp. 37-38

23 Ibid. quoting S. Benadava, "Las relaciones entre Derecho Internacional y Derecho Interno ante los Tribunales Chilenos" ["The Relationships Between International Law and Domestic Law Before the Chilean Courts"], in León S. (coordinator), *Nuevos Enfoques del Derecho Internacional [New Points of View in International Law]*, Editorial Jurídica de Chile, Santiago, 1992, p. 35.

24 Ibid., p. 38.

25 Ibid. quoting the 1980 Chilean Constitution article 82, No. 2.

26 Ibid., p. 38.

27 Universal Declaration, Article 3.

28 Covenant on Civil and Political Rights, Articles 6.1 y 9.1.

29 Convention of Belém do Pará, Articule 1, 2(b) y 4.

30 American Human Rights Convention, Article 1.

31 Chilean Republic, 1980 Political Constitution, Editorial Jurídica de Chile, Santiago, 1992, Article 19(1) (hereinafter "Chilean Constitution"). It is important to underscore that this same article says, "The law protects the lives of the unborn." Ibid. Together with laws that prohibit abortion in

all cases, this provision of the Constitution can be read to mean that the State chooses to protect the right of "the unborn" over the life of the pregnant woman, thus violating the woman's right to life.

32 See paragraph 106(k) of the Beijing Platform (recommending that laws that penalize women for abortion be reviewed.)

33 Rebecca Cook, International Human Rights and Women's Reproductive Health, 24 *Studies in Family Planning*, p. 73, 79 (1993).

34 Concluding Observations of the Human Rights Committee: Peru, 18/11/96.CCPR/C/79/Add.72. (concluding observations/comments), paragraph 15.

35 Ibid., paragraph 22.

36 Stanley Henshaw, "How safe is theraputic abortion?" in *Pregnancy Termination and Labor*, Parthenon, 1991.

37 WHO, Maternal Health and Safe Motherhood Program, *Abortion*, p. 12 (1994).

38 UNFPA, *The State of World Population*, p. 23 (1997).

39 Stephen Isaacs, J.D., "Aborto Clandestino vs. Aborto Regulado, En Algunos Países del Mundo"("Clandestine Abortion vs. Regulated Abortion in Certain Countries of the World"), in *El Aborto en Chile: Elementos Para el Debate* [*Abortion in Chile: Elements for Debate*], p. 36, Corporación de Salud y Políticas Sociales [Corporation for Health and Social Policy], 1996.

40 Ibid. citing Paxman, John et al., "The Clandestine Epidemic: The Practice of Unsafe Abortion in Six Latin Amerian Countries," in *International Family Planning Perspectives*, July-August 1993, pp. 205-224, table 4.

41 The Alan Guttmacher Institute, *Aborto clandestino: Una realidad latinoamericana* [*Clandestine Abortion: A Latin American Reality*], p. 24, 1994.

42 Stephen Isaacs, J.D., "Aborto Clandestino vs. Aborto Regulado, En Algunos Países del Mundo" ["Clandestine Abortion vs. Regulated Abortion in Certain Countries of the World"], op. cit., p. 36.

43 Ibid. quoting Stanley Henshaw, "Induced Abortions: A World Review, 1990", *Family Planning Perspectives*, p. 78, table 2.

44 Covenant on Civil and Political Rights, Article 9. See also the American Convention on Human Rights, Article 4.

45 María Isabel Rosas Ballinas, *Aborto por Violación: Dilemas Éticos y Jurídicos* [*Abortion after Rape: Ethical and Legal Dilemmas*], p. 50, DEMUS and the Population Council, 1997.

46 Cairo Programme of Action, paragraph 6.6.

47 See the section: The evolution of reproductive Rights as Human Rights.

48 Women's Convention, Article 2(g).

49 Rebecca J. Cook, "International Protection of Women's Reproductive Rights," in 24 International Law and Politics, p. 698, 1992.

50 See the Women's Convention, art. 2; Covenant on Civil and Political Rights, art. 2; and the Covenant on Economic and Social Rights, art. 2.

51 Universal Declaration, Article 25(1).

52 Covenant on Economic and Social Rights, Article 12(1).

53 Chilean Constitution, Article 19(9).

54 Women's Convention, Article 12.1.

55 Ibid., Article 14.2.

56 Ibid., Article 16.1.

57 Cairo Programme of Action, ¶8.25; Beijing Platform, ¶106(k).

58 Rosas Ballinas, *Aborto por Violación: Dilemas Éticos y Jurídicos* [*Abortion after Rape: Ethcial and Legal Dilemmas*], op. cit., p. 29-31.

59 No contraceptive method is 100% effective. For example, even when used properly, diaphragms have a failure rate of 6%, and condoms of 3%. Moreover, the use of these methods is usually not perfect, resulting in an even higher failure rate. *Institute of Medicine, Contraceptive Research and Development: Looking to the Future*, vol. I, table 3-1, 1996. Furthermore, some studies have demonstrated that the effectiveness of temporary contraceptive methods also depends on the users' circumstances. Those women who know the correct use and the secondary effects of a contraceptive method have a better chance of using the method effectively. National Research Council and Institute of Medicine, *Developing New Contraceptives*, pp. 22-23, 1990.

60 Covenant on Civil and Political Rights, Article 17.1.

61 Chilean Constitution, Article 19.4.

62 See *Constitución, Tratados y Derechos Esenciales* [*Constitution, Treaties and Essential Rights*], Cecilia Medina, ed., Corporación Nacional de Reparación y Reconciliación [National

Corporation for Reparation and Reconciliation], Santiago, 1993.

63 This kind of pretrial imprisonment is called "preventive imprisonment" because it is supposed to prevent the defendant from being a menace to society, or endangering the victim of the crime, or obstructing the judge's investigation. Judges evaluate the level of "danger" posed by the defendant to determine whether to grant or deny release on bail. Judges consider the defendant's personality, personal characteristics, and the nature of the crime. Therefore, persons with criminal records are usually held in preventive imprisonment, as are those suspected of committing certain crimes. Preventive imprisonment in the Chilean criminal justice system should be an exception, since it limits a protected right, the right to liberty.

64 The Covenant on Civil and Political Rights in its Article 9 (3) states: "Anyone arrested or detained on a criminal charge shall be brought promptly before a judge or other officer authorized by law to exercise judicial power and shall be entitled to trial within a reasonable time or to release. It shall not be the general rule that persons awaiting trial shall be detained in custody, but release may be subject to guarantees to appear for trial, at any other stage of the judicial proceedings, and, should occasion arise, for execution of the judgement."

65 American Convention on Human Rights, Article 8(2).

66 Article 19(7)(e) says: "Pretrial release from custody shall apply, unless the judge considers the individual's detention or preventive imprisonment to be necessary for the investigation or for the victim's or society's safety. " Chile, *Criminal Procedure Code*, 13th edition, Editorial Jurídica de Chile, Santiago, 1995 (hereafter, "Criminal Procedure Code").

67 See Articles 275 and 277, *Criminal Procedure Code*.

68 Humberto Nogueira, Emilio Pfeffer and Mario Verdugo, *Derecho Consitucional, Tomo I* [*Consititutional, Law Volume I*], p. 203, Editorial Jurídica de Chile, Santiago, 1994. The *Consejo de Estado* is the highest administrative court in the country. Like most Latin American countries, Chile has a system of courts parallel to the civil and criminal courts called administrative courts. They are charged with matters where the state is the defendant. The *Consejo de Estado* functions both as a court of appeal for this system and as a consultative body for the government on constitutional matters.

69 Neville Blanc, Humberto Nogueira, Emilio Pfeffer and Mario Verdugo, *La Constitución Chilena, Tomo I* [*Chilean Consititution, Volume I*], p. 126, Centro de Estudios y Asistencia Legislativa, Univesidad Católica de Valparaiso, [Center for Legal Aid and Studies, Catholic University of Valparaiso], 1992.

70 Nogueira. et al., 1994, op.cit., p 201

71 Josefina Hurtado, "Programas Estatales de Salud Dirigidos Hacia las Mujeres: Imágenes de Mujer y Lógicas de Acción" ["State Programs for Women: Images and Motivations for Action"] in *Sexualidad y Reproducción Hacia la Construcción de Derechos* [*Sexuality and Reproduction: Towards the Construction of Rights*], p.27-28, CORSAPS, 1994.

72 Ibid.

73 Ibid.

74 Ibid.

75 *Yearbook of Hospital Expenses* 1983, 1984, 1990 and 1991, National Statistics Institute, published in various years.

76 Orellana, et al. quoted by George Acasadi, Gwendolyn Johnson-Acasadi and Michael Vlassoff, *La maternidad sin riesgos en América Latina y el Caribe: aspectos socio-culturales y demográficos de la salud materna*, [*Riskless Maternity in Latin America and the Caribbean: sociocultural and demographic aspects of maternal health*], p. 28, translated by Paul Constance, Family Care International, New York, 1993.

77 Stanley Henshaw, "How safe is therapeutic abortion?" in *Pregnancy Termination and Labor*, Vol. 5, p. 39, 1991 (Proceedings of the XIIIth World Congress of Gynecology and Obstetrics, Singapore, Sept. 1991).

78 Molina Lopez, Orellana et. al. "Características del aborto en Chile" ["Characteristics of Abortion in Chile"], in *Cuadernos Médico Sociales* [*Social and Medical Notebooks*], Vol. XIX, No. 1, p. 9, Santiago, 1978.

79 See Gloria Salazar, *Acción sobre el aborto inducido mediante el apoyo integral a la mujer post abortante* [*Action to Combat Induced Abortion through Comprehensive Support to Women Post-abortion*], Instituto de la Mujer [Institute for

Women], Santiago, 1993.
80 Patricio Gayán, "Consecuencias médicas del aborto inducido en Chile" [Medical Consequences of Abortion in Chile"], in *Aborto inducido en Chile* [*Induced Abortion in Chile*], p. 49, ed. Mariano Requena, Sociedad Chilena de Salud Pública, Santiago, 1990.
81 Oladipo Oladipo, "Preventing and Managing Complications of Induced Abortion in Third World Countries," in *International Journal of Gynecology & Obstetrics, Women's Health in the Third World: The Impact of Unwanted Pregnancy*, Ireland, 1989, p. 26.
82 Ibid.
83 Mario Verdugo Marincovich, *Código Penal, Tomo III*, 2ª edición, Editorial Jurídica ConoSur Ediar, Santiago, 1986, p. 697 and following.
84 Open Forum on Reproductive Rights and Health, *Simposio Nacional: Leyes para la Salud y la Vida de las Mujeres. Hablemos de Aborto Terapéutico* [*National Symposium: Laws for Women's Health and Life: Let's Talk About Therapeutic Abortion*], 1993.
85 Article 19 (1) says: "The Constitution ensures all persons: 1. The right to life...The law protects the life of the unborn."
86 See Criminal Code, art. 15.
87 See Criminal Code, art. 16.
88 See Criminal Code, art. 17.
89 Legal and sociological definitions are not necessarily the same. Thus, both women who have an abortion and abortion providers are considered principals when they concur in the abortion procedure. Likewise, accomplices and accessories to a crime can be so either in relation to the woman having an abortion or to the abortion provider. In this report, both types of definitions will be used depending upon the issue being underscored.
90 This information should be taken as indicating a trend, not as exact figures. Each court gives its figures directly to the National Statistics Insititute (NSI), and they may be erroneous. In fact, errors occur because many courts do not distinguish between incoming cases and cases pending from previous years. Information on cases pending is collected by the NSI as a separate entry, and is not published, although the Ministry of Justice receives a copy. Thus, it was possible to determine that by the end of the 1980s the number of pending cases was significant. The NSI started a new system in 1990, giving the courts time to close pending cases. Thus, that year's figures are not yet available.
91 The other entity empowered to bring those suspected of crimes before criminal justice authorities are the *Carabineros*, another policing body. The statistics kept by this institution do not distinguish between crimes, thus making it impossible to use their statistics on those detained.
92 Criminal Procedure Code, Article 81.
93 A complaint consists of reporting criminal behavior to a court, usually with the intention of taking a part in the trial, as distinct from just reporting the crime. The petition by the Attorney General's Office is a rare way of starting a criminal process.
94 Chilean Constitution, Article 19.
95 Criminal Code, Article 247(2).
96 Criminal Procedure Code, Article 201(2).
97 Criminal Procedure Code, Article 84(5).
98 Criminal Procedure Code, Article 494 (9).
99 Doctor Roberto Von Bennewitz holds that physicians are obligated by their triple status as citizen, health professional, and public officials. See Chilean Medical Profesionals Association, "Panel: Therapeutic Abortion," *Working Notebooks No. 4*, Medical Work and Group Action, p.5. Santiago, 1989 [Colegio Médico de Chile, "Panel: Aborto Terapéutico," *Cuadernos de Trabajo Nº 4*, Departamento Trabajo Médico y Acción Gremial], p. 5, Santiago, 1989. To read a forensic doctor's position similar to that of criminal law scholar Alfredo Etcheberry see: Hernán Silva, *Medicina Legal y Psiquiatría Forense, Tomo II* [*Forensic Medicine and Forensic Psychiatry, Volume II*], p. 615 and following, Editorial Jurídica de Chile, Santiago, 1995.
100 Alfredo Etcheberry is a renowed criminal law scholar in Chile, and teaches at the Universidad de Chile.
101 Alfredo Etcheberry, *Derecho Penal, Tomo IV Parte Especial* [*Criminal Law part II, Volume IV, Special Section*] 2nd edition, p. 205, Editora Nacional Gabriela Mistral, Santiago, 1976.
102 Ibid.
103 Eduardo Novoa Monreal is a renowed criminal law scholar in Chile and an ex-president of the State Defense Council under President Salvador Allende.

104 The case of the medical files of the Chloe Clinic was appealed to the Supreme Court, which upheld the defense that the doctors were not obligated to and, in fact, were exempted from handing over the medical files of patients being prosecuted. See *Revista Fallos del Mes [Monthly Case Digest]*, No. 362, Jan. 1989.

105 The Chilean term is *pololo,* indicating a circumstantial amorous liaison.

106 One study shows that around 30% of criminal cases have public defenders providing the defense, mostly in those places where there are no Legal Aid Corporations. Correa y Jiménez, "Acceso de los Pobres a la Justicia" ["Access of the Poor to Justice"], in *Acceso de los Pobres a la Justicia [Access of the Poor to Justice]*, p. 136, ed. Franz Vanderschueren and Enrique Oviedo, Ediciones SUR, Santiago, 1995. These lawyers have no supervision and, in general, are young lawyers who have no more than two years of professional experience.

107 Cristán Riego, "El Proceso Penal Chileno y los Derechos Humanos, Vol. I" ["The Chilean Criminal Process and Human Rights, Vol. 1"], in *Aspectos Jurídicos, Cuaderno de Análisis Jurídico [Legal Aspects, Legal Analysis Journal]*, p. 78, Escuela de Derecho, Universidad Diego Portales, 1994.

108 If there are strong indications that a suspect under arrest participated in a crime, the judge may order a "processing decree," previously known as an "imprisonment decree." This decree is very important in the criminal process, because it starts the investigation and eventually could result in an indictment. A suspect can be detained up to five days for most crimes, without the need for a "processing decree." Once the "procesing decree" is issued, and the suspect remains in prison, it is considered "preventive imprisonment." In this case the suspect may ask, with or without the assistance of an attorney, for release. For an analysis of the human rights violations that occur as a result of preventive imprisonment, see the chapter Abortion and Human Rights.

109 See, e.g., Cristian Riego, "La Prision Preventiva" ["Preventive Imprisonment"], in *Cuaderno de Análisis Jurídico [Journal of Legal Analysis]*, Escuela de Derecho, Universidad Diego Portales, Santiago; María Angélica Jiménez, "El Proceso Penal chileno y los Derechos Humanos, Vol. II ["The Chilean Criminal Process and Human Rights, Vol. II"] in *Estudios Empíricos, Cuaderno de Análisis Jurídico [Empirical Studies, Legal Analysis Journal]*, Escuela de Derecho, Universidad Diego Portales, Santiago, 1994.

110 Criminal Code article 344 provides: "The woman who caused her own abortion or allowed another person to cause it will be punished with lesser imprisonment of the highest degree. If she did it to hide her dishonor, she will be punished with lesser imprisonment of medium degree."

111 See Criminal Procedure Code, Article 408(3).

112 The Institute of Forensic Medicine is an auxiliary of the judicial branch, and is empowered by the law to deal with all medical-forensic matters.

113 Criminal Procedure Code, Article 409 N° 1.

114 Criminal Procedure Code, Article 409 N° 5.

115 Molina, et. al., "Características del Aborto en Chile" ["Characteristics of Abortion in Chile"], op. cit., p. 17.

116 Gustavo González, "Chile: More Women but Less Time for Gender Debate," Interpress Service, Jan. 2 ,1998; Howard LaFranchi, "Chile May Allow Divorce to Snip Those Ties that Bind," *The Christian Science Monitor*, p. 6, December 30, 1997.

117 Mariana Ayluin and Ignacio Walker, *Familia y Divorcio, Razones de una Posición [Family and Divorce: Reasons for an Opinion]*, p. 33 (1996).

118 Benjamín Viel and Cristián Pereda, "El Embarazo No Deseado," ["Unwanted Pregnancy"] in *Cuadernos Médico-Sociales [Journal of Medicine and Society]*, XXXII, 4, 1991, p. 33.

119 The Alan Guttmacher Institute, *Aborto clandestino: Una realidad latinoamericana [Clandestine Abortion: A Latin American Reality]*, op. cit., p. 25.

120 Viel and Pereda, "El Embarazo No Deseado" ["Unwanted Pregnancy"] op. cit., p. 35.